W9-AHV-381

The New
Sales
Manager's
Survival
Guide

David A. Stumm

The New Sales Manager's Survival Guide

American Management Association

This book is available at a special
discount when ordered in bulk quantities.
For information, contact Special Sales Department,
AMACOM, a division of American Management Association,
135 West 50th Street, New York, NY 10020.

Library of Congress Cataloging in Publication Data

Stumm, David Arthur.
    The new sales manager's survival guide.

    Includes index.
    1. Sales management. I. Title.
HF5438.4.S88   1985   658.8'1   84-45787
ISBN 0-8144-5799-1

© 1985 AMACOM, a division of
American Management Association, New York.
All rights reserved.
Printed in the United States of America.

This publication may not be reproduced,
stored in a retrieval system,
or transmitted in whole or in part,
in any form or by any means, electronic,
mechanical, photocopying, recording, or otherwise,
without the prior written permission of AMACOM,
a division of American Management Association,
135 West 50th Street, New York, NY 10020.

Printing number

10 9 8 7 6 5 4 3 2 1

To my own
personal survival guide:
My **wife**

In the Beginning . . .

Perhaps I have been one of the more fortunate ones. I made my transition from salesman to sales manager after spending some five years as manager of sales training, corporate marketing staff. During that time, I had the opportunity to observe the sales world as well as the world of the sales manager from a vantage point seldom seen except in retrospect. Thus, by the time I had my first sales district, I had already been indoctrinated with the theory and principles of such courses as "Management Functions and Policies," "Marketing Management," "Management Techniques," "Advanced Management," and the rest. The bookshelves of my office were lined with a broad array of the known knowledge regarding the art of managing. I had merely to step in and do it.

Here I am, 15 light-years later—the product of sales management positions in several industries, the broadening experience that comes from working with many diverse sales and sales management groups as a sales training consultant, and the experience of returning to the active world of the sales manager in a reorganized division of a major industrial corporation. There have been many successes, and throughout I have had the opportunity to use all the knowledge, skills, and techniques that we will discuss herein.

Yet when the editors at AMACOM proposed a book directed at the needs of the new sales manager—a book I wholeheartedly agreed was vitally important and needed—I hesitated to begin.

How do you write about something as broad-based as management or managers and say anything meaningful?

My first book, *An Introduction to Sales Engineering*, published by Westinghouse, was written 20 minutes at a time while waiting to see buyers. I wrote to myself and for myself because I was searching for answers that I could not find in books or in the sales training courses I had attended. I wanted to know why some sales failed and why some sales succeeded. It seemed a lot of salesmen and sales managers were looking for the same answers to the same questions, because that book went through ten printings. It was a book written by a questing salesman to other questing salesmen.

By 1981, I had the answers, and I put them into another book, which was published by AMACOM, *Advanced Industrial Selling*. It was a salesman's book written to salesmen. From its pages came any number of letters, phone calls, and requests for speeches and seminars from the many who read it and also found within those pages what they wanted to know about the techniques of professional selling. I knew why salespeople succeeded and why they failed, and that book was written salesman to salesman.

Now I am asked to write for the new sales manager—manager-to-manager advice on how to win at a different game than we had all grown up being good at.

We have all observed sales managers, and we have observed their results. There are effective managers who are inefficient and efficient managers who are ineffective. What makes the efficient *and* effective sales manager? How does the new sales manager learn what has to be done to be effective in this chosen career? To arrive at an answer to such questions, this book needed a plan. The more I thought about the subject, the more I became aware that while there was a place to begin, unfortunately, there was no end to any discussion of the sales manager's job.

Thus, this book starts where it logically should, even with a step 1, step 2 approach. It begins with the logic of knowing what is needed first because one knows where it should go. It starts with a question, "What do I do first?" From that point on, it all comes together, so that every action of management is dependent on another coming before it or after it. You start—and the result is what matters. Since all travelers need a road map to guide them, this book serves that purpose for the new sales manager.

The Format We Will Follow

We should never measure activity, only results. Thus, in Chapter 1, I will attempt to answer the question of where the manager begins by looking at the very basic premise of determining what is known versus what is unknown in meeting the objectives of the sales unit. I have termed it, simply, the "gap" approach. In other words, all management thinking, and thus direction, will go toward filling this "gap"—toward producing results.

The sales managers can be only as effective in meeting those objectives as the people who report to them. In Chapter 2, we will examine the process of interviewing and hiring those salespeople who will play such an important role. This is not the digression it might at first appear to be. Selection can come into play at any time. I have therefore given it an important position at the beginning.

Chapter 3 then continues from where we left our thoughts at the end of Chapter 1. The objectives established for sales managers by their superiors must be met in the synergism of the combined objectives of their sales force. The objectives set for the individual salespeople have meaning only insofar as they contribute to the whole. Each objective must relate to what needs to be accomplished by each salesperson in closing his or her individual "gap." However, the art of meaningful objectives only demands that we move on and not stand still at this juncture. The goals that have been set become results only with careful nurturing. Thus, in Chapter 4, we continue what was started as we discuss the concepts and skills of supervising and controlling.

Chapter 5 becomes a logical point at which to examine the concepts of management by objectives, and then, to add a capstone to the previous chapters, we discuss the use of MBO as an effective management tool in measuring and rewarding the individual efforts and results of the sales force—the principles of management by objectives integrated fully with the elements of the corporate appraisal system.

Essentially, we could have stopped at this point and considered that what had been covered included all the functions necessary to the new sales manager. However, there is a chasm between what can be termed satisfactory and what can be termed professional. In Chapters 6 and 7, the discussion pursues the fine art of the sales manager as a team builder. Thus, we need to understand how the manager goes about this task and the role his or her own style of managing plays in the result.

At this point in the book, we will digress and examine some of the complementary functions and issues that are also important contributors to management success. In Chapters 8 and 9, I have combined the ins and outs of running a meeting with the function of sales training and the sales training meeting.

Finally, for sales managers to completely fulfill the role of the achiever of results through others, they need to understand success in selling. Fully understanding success means understanding failure. Chapter 10 explores the major reasons why salespeople fail and, more important, what some corrective actions might be.

Then, since a premise of this book is that the individual pieces do not stand alone, I have, in the final chapter, attempted to make some sense of each piece by putting them all together.

The Commitment to the Past

I have not written solely about my own experiences. Every example presented in this book is someone's true story. Many are personal; many more I saw happening around me. The principles and concepts discussed are not mine. They all come from teachers, peers, and managers I have had the opportunity to meet, talk to, and follow. Even the management tools presented are not wholly mine but evolved from the needs and the experiences of those who came before me. Yet this is how we all learn and grow.

As the examples, concepts, and management ideas poured themselves onto these pages, a hundred faces began to come alive again—faces from the past. They say you owe most of your own management style to the style exhibited by your first bosses. Writing that line I can only think of Dick Stowe, Merrill Peters, Joe Owsley, Fyre Ayers, and all the others from those early days at Westinghouse. I have to say thank you.

There were so many others along the way. Professional managers never stop learning and thus are forever indebted to some others whose guiding influence had more of an effect on continued growth than was perhaps realized at the time. All of the many managers from my past have contributed in their own individual ways to what I know and am. This, then, is as much the story of their successful fulfillment of the management experience as my own, and to all of them I dedicate this effort. They were all my teachers. Again, thank you.

The View from the
Front of the Roller Coaster

I have attempted to write a "how-to" book, not merely stating problems and what one "ought to do" about them but placing the experiences of those who have themselves faced these same problems into an understandable frame of reference that will help the manager newly struggling with those same problem areas. My objective throughout has been to bring the concepts and principles of sales management into the arena of common understanding in such a manner as to be not only thought-provoking but a guide to the very survival of the new sales manager.

I have found a strong tendency throughout to discuss a potential problem area as if there were one specific and all-enlightening solution to that situation. Yet I realize that can never be the case. My purpose is solely to help my readers think their way through each situation, and in this effort, I am mindful of the words of that first boss, Merrill Peters, when he said:

> Managing is very like the performer who keeps all those plates spinning on the ends of a row of sticks. You never have a single problem, or a single objective. . . . If you want to make a career of managing, then you'd better learn to deal with uncertainty, and with situations and problems that are never really solved once and for all. Most of the time you'll go home feeling as though all your plates are slowing down at once.

Bearing in mind that my female colleagues take pride in being called "good salesmen," I use the term to refer to both men and women, and use the terms salesmen and salesperson interchangeably. I hope the reader will overlook the use of masculine pronouns; I find it awkward to repeatedly refer to "he or she." I recognize that women are playing a growing role in sales and management. I believe that management carries no gender, but language is resistant to change.

Finally, I do not assume that I have covered all the sales manager's possible problem areas, but I have certainly dealt with those that appear to be most important and recurring. Nor do I mean to imply that these problems are the exclusive province of the sales manager. I write about what I have been for the past 15 years of my career—a sales manager above all else.

All managers, whatever the function, are problem solvers. That is perhaps the primary purpose for their existence. In 1968, I had the privilege of hearing Dr. Norman Vincent Peale speak at a gathering at the Pittsburgh Hilton Hotel in which he said, ". . . problems make strong men . . . the positive thinker is not afraid of a problem . . . every problem contains the seeds of its own solution. The only way to go forward is by the problem route." With these thoughts in mind, let's go forward.

David Arthur Stumm

Contents

Chapter 1
Getting Started:
What Do I Do First?
1

Chapter 2
Staffing Up:
How Do I Get What I Need?
24

Chapter 3
Setting Objectives:
What Objectives Are Meaningful?
49

Chapter 4
Supervision and Control:
How Do I Keep It Going?
68

Chapter 5
The Appraisal System:
Is This Really Necessary?
98

Chapter 6
The Case for Team Building:
What Makes One Group More Effective Than Another?
114

Chapter 7
Developing Your Management Style:
How Can I Motivate My Sales Force?
132

Chapter 8
Running a Sales Meeting:
Why Not Just Call the Nearest Hotel?
156

Chapter 9
Training the Sales Force:
What Makes an Effective Sales Program?
175

Chapter 10
Why Salespeople Fail:
Can I Do Anything?
195

Chapter 11
Putting It All Together
216

Index
229

The New
Sales
Manager's
Survival
Guide

1

Getting Started: What Do I Do First?

So they made you a manager? Welcome to the great management crapshoot! And unless you are one of the very fortunate few who have received some specific training for the role, you are going to be asking yourself, "What do I do first?" "Where do I begin?"

Unfortunately, you are also going to be very busy getting involved in your new position, with people to meet—staff, peers, customers—and your own sales force. Then there are all the computer runs to study, past reports giving you some feel for what went before, and of course, all the current reports that just will not wait for you to catch up before they become due. I said, "unfortunately" because you are going to be too busy to take the time to sit quietly by yourself and ask, "Where do I start? What does being a manager mean?" You are going to be too busy just being one.

However, assuming that the moment does arrive, you now need some advice. That is what this book is all about—a manager-to-manager discussion about the job of running a sales force, or region or district, area or country. This is a serious book. It is a manual for survival in the modern corporate world directed specifically to the needs of the sales manager. It is going to look at the problems of being a sales manager. It is advice for the sales manager from a sales manager.

1

Within these pages, I have attempted to capture the theory and principles of sales management based on the successes, and the failures, of real sales managers who have had to face the same conflicts, problems, and questions you now face as you begin your latest swim in the shark-infested waters of the business world. The analogy is quite apt, since within those waters lie any number of competitive situations, both inside and outside the company, that could trigger the end of a hitherto successful career. It is a basic premise of this book that the key ingredient for managerial survival lies in the ability of managers to understand what is going on around them, to know how to harness the strengths and weaknesses of those for whom they are responsible, to communicate effectively with those to whom they are in turn responsible, and above all, to know where they want to go and how they are going to get there.

This is also a "how-to" book. I feel that in this manager-to-manager discussion, it is not enough to say simply, "This is what you should do," or even to explain why you should do it. You need to see some concrete examples of how it can be done.

Let's Get Started

I recall someone once describing management as "crossing over a bridge," the implication being that until you have actually made the transition from sales rep to sales manager, you will really not understand it. Perhaps fortunately, it is the person who is good at sales who gets the promotion, as you know. Without this qualification, there is no upward progress. But the "good" salesman achieved that success as a doer, not a director. You are a manager today because you have proved your ability to accomplish goals as a salesman. You were a good salesman, and you were asked to cross that bridge and become something else.

If there is a single reason managers fail, it lies in this: that having crossed over, they continue to do what made them successful in the first place. They continue to be salesmen, and thus become supersalesmen, but in the process, they fail to become managers.

I am not going to define management for you. It has been done many times, and by experts. Also, I am not sure any definition will really add to what I am going to present. Instead of thinking about what management is or where it is going, let's see how it gets there (which in sum total is the subject of this book). And in doing so, perhaps you will see why as a new manager you may feel some confusion and frustration over the best way to get started in the job.

Perhaps I can best begin by sorting out where this feeling of frustration comes from, and to do so we have to keep in mind three areas of potential conflict:

1. Your own personal "change index" as you go from doing to directing.
2. Your preparation for the job of being a manager.
3. Your attitude, which gives you the flexibility to adapt to different situations you will face in your career as a manager.

Now I Am a Manager!

Simplistically speaking, you are in your position to fulfill two purposes: (1) communication, (2) direction. That's it! That's *all* of it! And as you will see in just a moment, these two purposes are closely related, almost interchangeable.

The reason you are in your present position is because somebody (your present boss or your boss's boss) thinks you are qualified to serve those two purposes. Maybe you are not feeling particularly qualified right at the moment, but you were chosen because you are the best there is, given your background, training, accomplishments, and readiness and, most important, because it was felt that you will serve those purposes without embarrassing anyone.

Communication

Organizations—from the most basic (the two-person, employer-employee) all the way to the largest and most complex—have the common problem of passing down the wishes, goals, desires, and hopes from the top and passing up the discoveries, facts, feelings, and insights from those on the firing line. Yet as a consultant friend once observed, "The myth of communication is the assumption that there is any."

Behavior specialists tell us that your first boss will have an indelible influence on the way you will someday manage. For better or worse, you have unconsciously studied how to approach the function of managing, and particularly if your managerial role model's approach to managing appeared successful, you will find your own style closely reflecting that person's.

> I remember my first boss as a young salesman in Cincinnati selling industrial apparatus for Westinghouse. M. K. "Pete" Peters had an easygoing manner that seemed to encourage those under him to make decisions, accept the risk of doing something on their own, and think through what had been done. Yet he was always there when you moved too far or too fast. He encouraged you to act but just as quickly seemed to sense when you were in over your head. It was also evident, though, that he did not treat any two of us the same. It was as though he instinctively understood the differences in each of his salespeople and reacted to what each one wanted and needed. Because of this, each of us was allowed to stretch and grow at whatever rate we ourselves were most comfortable with. Some of us pushed harder than others. Some he eased up on and led by the hand.
>
> I remember a moment following a long string of questions I had been asking him. Some seemed rather basic, and I asked, "Do you mind all these questions?" He said, "Dave, that's how I can tell you're progressing. When all the questions you ask are those I can't answer, you'll be ready for my job."
>
> Occasionally, giving some of us our heads created a problem. There was the time a miscalculation on my part resulted in a $500 error—a good sum in those days. I was embarrassed, to say the least, particularly since I felt I had let Pete down. In reprimand, he said, "What did you learn?" and we had a discussion about that instead of the chewing out I had thought I would get. To my mind, it was a lot more effective than any other approach would have been.

What's my point? That my early experiences as a salesman taught me to be comfortable with challenge. Because I could observe the results of people-oriented management on my actions and growth, I found it easier to apply these same principles to others when I began to manage. The growth in my own professional "change index" allowed an easy transition from doing to directing.

Regardless of your own experience, your future as a manager begins with your ability to accept the fact that when you crossed that bridge from salesman to manager, you accepted the need to change roles, and to change roles drastically, from the role of receiver of interpreted information called "company policy and goals" to the role of interpreter of those policies.

> There was a salesman, let's call him Tom, who just could not get a report in either on time or complete. That included expense reports, call reports, monthly reports—everything. Fortunately for Tom, he was also a very consistent 120 percent of quota month after month. After a period of frustrating myself over the situation, I said, "Tom, I'll make you a deal. As long as you are ahead of quota I'll quit bugging you for any report except keeping up to date with the expense report. But the minute you fall below 100 percent, I want every single report not only on time, but anticipated." Not only was it an arrangement that worked very well for both of us, but I suspect it was a major incentive in keeping Tom ahead of his quota. But that's another chapter.

Now I could have reacted in two other ways. For one, I could have interpreted company policy as demanding an inflexible adherence to the filing of those reports and used a lot of energy forcing compliance week after week, month after month. On the other hand, I could have caved in and made no demands at all on Tom. I could, in effect, have shown him that he was right. Also, that would have been the easy way.

However, more to the point is getting you to accept the change in role in your new job—getting you to accept the difference in outlook between what you have hitherto been successful at doing and what is now more critical to your continued success. Now you must weigh each action on all those others to whom you have a responsibility as a manager. As a salesman you had a responsibility only to yourself for your actions. This means a change in your role. That you do change is vital, both to your success and to the success of all those over whom you are now placed in a position of authority. It is a matter of your attitude toward this role change. Your attitude will have a major effect on what you will accomplish.

Your boss and all the bosses above you have the same concerns for that communication pattern—both up and down—as you have. What is really important, however, is not the ability to communicate but the style of the manager making the communication. A lot depends on the style used, as we will be discussing later.

Direction

Direction has to do with seeing that the objectives, rules, procedures, and all other processes of administration of a sales force that come down (both to you and from you) are carried out effectively. As we have already observed, if you've been a successful salesman, it is sometimes much easier just to do what has to be done yourself than to direct its being done. But that is not managing.

The direction, or "getting things done," part of the job is where the manager has the most freedom to develop a style. At the same time, for most newly appointed managers, the feeling of frustration that comes from the "What do I do now?" environment is created by the very fact that what must be done is not handed to them in the form of a list of standard operating procedures.

There are, of course, many rules and procedures, formal and informal, in every company—rules that say, "You will submit an expense account every week or every month"; "You will meet your quota or turn in a report explaining why not"; "You will drive this kind of a company car"; "You will fly coach whenever possible"; "Your salesmen will contact, sell, and maintain customer relations"; and so on and so on. But such rules do not tell you how you get your people to comply or what is the best time or manner in which to do it. That is up to you. All you need to know is that it is very important for your survival that you do it somewhat effectively; also, that you do not break any other rules or laws while you are doing it and that none of your supervisors are embarrassed by what you do while accomplishing it. But then, the reason you are in the job, as I said, is because your bosses felt you could do it—even if they bite their nails more than they used to while you get on with it.

More managers fail because they do not grasp the idea behind the purpose of their position than for any other reason. They become frustrated, either through a misunderstanding that it is up to them to create the "how to" (the direction) or because there are no "ten steps" to doing so.

For some years now, I have had the fun and the challenge of teaching an advanced management course at a local college, and I am continually taken aback by the number of students, even those coming from business careers who expect a management course to give them concrete answers to the management problems being presented. They feel they can somehow learn a magic formula they can apply to the job of managing. Remember from your selling that there were no "ten steps to close" there, either. Selling was easy in terms of concepts and techniques, but people are complex. People are what you were there to sell to, and now they are what you are there to manage. That is why it is sometimes much easier to just do it yourself. But if you become the supersalesman your subordinates will not grow. They will stay dependent—and that is not what you are there to achieve.

Getting Ready to Manage

Now I am going to tell you what you should do first in your new job. I do not mean the first day you walk into your new office and your superior introduces you to your sales force. I do not even refer to those first hectic days you will spend pouring over the history in the files you have inherited trying to get a handle on things. It is even possible that you will have been on the job several months, but when the time comes that you are ready to sit back and think how you can "get organized," then you are ready to start managing.

Let's see where we are going with this so the process of getting there becomes clearer. Taking the objectives of your job in total, the overriding reason for your existence (spelled s-u-r-v-i-v-a-l) is to somehow find a way to eventually meet your sales target or at least maintain a reasonable, explainable, and justifiable movement toward it. Little else will be important in the long run. But first things first, and your first task is to establish and secure a beachhead. This means communicating—in this instance, not only down but up!

Find Out What Is Expected

There are few companies today that have not upgraded, or at least begun the process of upgrading, their personnel policies in recognition of the importance of human resources management. Those that are involved with such updated thinking have also dusted off their approach to management by objectives and have integrated these concepts into the company appraisal system.

In a later chapter, we are going to examine your role in working with an effective appraisal system with your own sales force. Right now, in this process of getting you properly launched as a sales manager, let's see how you can begin your career by putting the MBO system to work for you.

If you are one of the very rare newly appointed sales managers who had a boss who took you aside within the first few months and established a number of mutually agreed upon objectives with you, you can skip to the next section of this chapter. Time, however, has a neat way of getting away from all of us, and top managers are no exception. Therefore, I can assume one of two conditions exists for you:

1. Although your firm has a well-established MBO program, it has not played a major part in your getting started in your new job.
2. Your firm has no established program.

Whether you belong to either of the above groups is not important. You are about to create your own program.

At one time, while attending a workshop with a group of other managers, I heard one of our fellow participants, a marketing consultant, tell the following story, which made a profound impression on me at the time.

> George was involved with consulting for a midwest firm when the marketing director said to him, "You are going to be doing some traveling for us on this project, and when you get to Atlanta, I would like you to give me your opinion of the sales manager there. We hired him with the greatest of expectations, and . . . well, he just isn't working out. Maybe you could have a talk with him."
>
> George said he would and asked the director how he was judging this manager. "What objectives have you set for him?" "Objectives?" snapped the director. "He doesn't need any objectives. All he has to do is make his quota for the district!" With a little urging, the marketing director sat down and wrote out a list of objectives, which George put into his briefcase and left town.

As George recalled, by the time he met the Atlanta sales manager, he had forgotten the request and the list of objectives in his briefcase. But the manager was in such a state—"George, I don't know what they want. Seems everything I do is wrong!"—that George simply handed him the list of objectives and went home.

One year later, the marketing director called him. "George, I don't know what you did to that sales manager in Atlanta, but I want you to come back and do the same thing to all my managers. You remember that list of objectives I gave you? Well, he's met every one of them!"

George confessed he had given the manager the list. There was dead silence on the other end of the phone for a brief moment, and then the director said, "I knew it, he cheated!"

Funny? I get laughs with that story every time I speak to management groups. In truth, though, it is too real not to be rather tragic.

My point here is to say, "Don't get yourself in a similar position." Know what objectives have been set for you. Insist on it! How? Tomorrow morning (or Monday, if you read this on a weekend) pick up the phone or write to your boss and say:

> As I analyze what I have to get done, I have come up with the following list of three [or four or five or six—make them key, important, and to the point] objectives that I want to accomplish by the end of the quarter. I am sure you will have some other important ones that I may have missed. I think our mutual understanding in this area is important to my accomplishing what you want. Could I please have your thoughts and comments on this matter?

Then if you do not get a response in a reasonable time, call your boss. You need this feedback. When the quarter ends, send him a progress report—"I made the first three but missed my target on four and five, so I am extending them another quarter and adding these four new objectives. Could I please have your agreement?" When the time comes for the annual review, guess what will form the basis for your rating? But isn't that what management by objectives is all about?

Is it worthwhile?

I have a friend whose job description says, "Manage the assigned territory in a manner that will maximize performance." He was fired two years later because he wasn't "managing" the way his superior "thought" he ought to be, although the firm paid him a $10,000 bonus the month before his termination.

We will be discussing communication in terms of achieving your objectives—that is, communicating down—at a later point. Right now, because you want to put your beginning in as favorable a light as you can with your own boss, let's discuss one of the best techniques you have available to you to accomplish this.

Communicating Up!

One of the things that a manager both fears and dislikes is not knowing what is going on, being surprised with bad news, being caught off-guard. This is true at every level, including your own. That is a major reason for the emphasis I am going to place on upward communication. I bet you thought upward communication was for presenting market and sales data. It is, but passing market and sales data up is only one purpose of upward communication and, from a personal survival point of view, perhaps not even the most important.

Keeping your management "on top of things" should be the easiest aspect of the job. That is what all those reports you dislike pulling together every month are designed to do. But that is the formal side of communication. There is an informal route that is even more important because it expresses feelings, opinions, hopes, fears, and all the rest. It is called one-on-one communication, talking it over, kicking it around, or just plain "touching base" (as the advertising people like to say, "Let's run it up the flagpole and see who salutes!").

When you are all by yourself out there in a field sales office, it is not quite so easy, is it? That's why Mr. Bell invented the telephone. Make this rule for yourself: Never let a single week go by without calling your boss at least once. If you are really career-minded, that should also include the time you are on vacation.

I once had a boss who traveled so constantly and widely that finding him on the other end of a phone was exceedingly difficult and even rare. I started a handwritten memo system I termed "rambling." I would simply write, off the top of my head, while on a plane, having breakfast in a hotel, or just sitting late in the office. In these ramblings, I would tell him my feelings and my opinions about what I was doing, experiencing, observing, or wanted him to know. Because the communication was handwritten and personal, it did not demand a reply. It just kept him informed. And what a great way to plant ideas!

At this early stage of your "getting organized," what are you trying to communicate? You are telling your superior how you see things, your problems, opportunities, and most important, how you plan to start moving your sales force toward the targets set for them—your targets—and when! Perhaps you might even want to include "how," although at this point you probably do not know "how." But I am coming to that. Right now, the main objective you should have is to be certain you have the time to accomplish what you want to accomplish, and the best way to get this time is to have your boss in agreement with what you are doing and where you are headed. How is this for a note?

Jim:

Just to let you know some of my thoughts on a possible problem area I have run into during these past weeks. I know we both thought the negotiation with Hadley Machine Company was on target, but it appears Bob Jones is not as close to things as he has been reporting. As a matter of fact, I am beginning to wonder how effectively he is really covering his territory. In the next few weeks, I am going to be spending more time than is probably justified with Bob to see what the problem really might be, and I will make a few calls on my own around his territory. If you have any other thoughts on this, let me know what you would suggest.

Or, again:

Jim:

I have discussed individual territory objectives with each of my salesmen. As a matter of information, I am attaching a rough breakdown listing areas in each of the territories where I think we will have to make a concentrated effort to find additional customers. Right now, the list is fairly rough, but it will give you an idea of where I feel I am going to have to be putting my time if we are going to fill the "gap" between sales and objectives.

The "Gap" Approach

It is one thing to have objectives—for example, "Make $10 million in sales in the following product lines or industry categories." It is something else to know how you are going to do it and translate that to the sales force in the form of directions for them to follow. But let's see how we might go about this.

We will start by discussing a single sales territory. Although every territory is different, just as every industry is different, we can deal with the differences in all territories and in all industries by dealing with their similarities.

In general, the analysis of each territory will be consistent with respect to the specific relationship that territory has historically had with current sales trends, volumes, and quotas or objectives. In other words, the first thing to be determined comes from looking at each individual territory and asking two questions:

Where are current sales coming from?
Where do I find more to make up any deficit?

That is really all there is to it. Out of the search for answers to these questions will come something I have long referred to as the "gap" approach. Let me outline it for you.

I think I can explain this better with an example. Let's assume a sales territory with a quota of $1,000,000. Now suppose there are a number of major "knowns"—that is, customer renewable orders that are perhaps annual purchase contracts that will be renewed throughout the year with some reasonable assurance of their continuing. Let us assume that in the case of our selected territory, there are three such customers, whose annual contracts will amount to, say, $450,000.

Let's also assume that historically in this territory (last year, for example) there were enough small purchases to amount to a miscellaneous $50,000. Now, what we have is:

Objective		$1,000,000
Accounted for		
Known accounts	$450,000	
Miscellaneous accounts	50,000	
	$500,000	− 500,000

"Gap"—to be uncovered, negotiated,
    and closed $ 500,000

We will take this a step further and assume the following on-going sales efforts or negotiations, along with the estimated probability or chance of a successful closing within the target or objective period—in this instance, by the end of the current calendar year:

St. Clare	$200,000 (50 percent chance)
Torrence	$120,000 (75 percent chance)
Main Electric	$80,000 (60 percent chance)

Now, if we multiply the expected value of each negotiation by the probability of success, we have:

St. Clare	($200,000 × .50) =	$100,000
Torrence	($120,000 × .75) =	90,000
Main Electric	($80,000 × .60) =	48,000
		$238,000

We will then round off the $238,000 to $240,000. (It has always appeared to me rather missing the point to work with estimated figures and then carry them out to the nearest decimal point.)

Thus, recapping the previous example:

Objective		$1,000,000
Accounted for		
Known accounts	$450,000	
Miscellaneous accounts	50,000	
Current negotiations	240,000	
	$740,000	− 740,000
"Gap"		$ 260,000

The $260,000 "gap" must still be made up through the judicious search for new potential sales by the salesperson responsible for this particular territory. Your job, as sales manager, having determined what is needed, is to help the sales force close this "gap" between objective and knowns—or determine the reason why it cannot be done.

There are, obviously, some industries where all sales are negotiated on a "one-time" contract or order basis. For example, companies selling capital equipment would fall into such a category, as would companies selling supplies, although anytime you can predict a series of repeating sales, they become "knowns." Where this cannot be done accurately, it simply means that the known is literally reduced to zero, with perhaps not even a miscellaneous group. There is nothing but "gap" in such an example.

But before we finish, here are a couple of other examples. One features a multitude of product lines, and the other is from the world of intangible sales.

Joe Batton is a sales representative with Royal Electric Supply, selling a wide range of products to industrial users and some equipment manufacturers on the city's west side. Because of the variety of product lines, Joe categorizes his customers by type and also by some key products that fall into large, identifiable groups:

Objective		$1,000,000
Accounted for		
Renewable contracts	$200,000	
MRO buyers	350,000	
Key negotiations		
Control centers ($100,000 × 50 percent chance)	50,000	
MRO contracts (averaging 65 percent chance)	70,000	
Other negotiations (averaging 80 percent chance)	130,000	
	$800,000	−800,000
"Gap"		$200,000

Joanne Carleton works for a national laboratory selling a blood analysis service to physicians:

Objective		$500,000
Accounted for		
Renewable contracts	$300,000	
Current negotiations (averaging 40 percent chance)	120,000	
	$420,000	−420,000
"Gap"		$ 80,000

That is the theory, together with a number of examples that should show that it is applicable to all sales territories and all industries. Now let us see what we can do with this information. After all, that is what managing is all about—communicating and directing to achieve a result.

Sales effectiveness, as you surely have discovered, comes from using a rifle rather than a shotgun—in other words, identifying targets where your chances of hitting the bull's-eye are the best and going after those targets before others where your chances of success are slimmer. The effective sales force consists of people who have measured each prospect against their strengths and their weaknesses—strengths and weaknesses in product features, benefits, service, and company as well as in their personal abilities.

The "gap" approach is no more than this. It presents an organized way of looking at a salesman's territory and segregating the various elements on which to concentrate sales effort. Obviously, any territory with sufficient knowns to eliminate the "gap" presents different strategy demands than one that is all "gap." But we have to know what we are working with before we can develop a strategy to deal with it. What I have proposed is a method of cataloging the knowns and the unknowns in each territory.

Developing Territory Strategies

Now take a look at your sales force. Let's assume, for simplicity, that you have one brand new salesman, one who has been in the territory about two years, and one with several years' experience. In effect, what you have is a range of individual experiences and potentials, which are also going to be matched up in varying degrees with differing territory structures.

If we are going to turn this information into a workable tool, we now have to look at each of those salespeople individually in terms of the "gap" we have identified in each respective territory. So let us start with that new person.

Introducing Bill Thompson

Bill Thompson is the newest and youngest of your sales force, having been hired just weeks after your own appointment as sales manager. Bill's previous sales experience consists of approximately two years with a local electrical distributor. Bill has a degree in marketing from a reputable trade school. He was hired to replace Ted Manning, who had been discharged after some three years of mediocre effort, which left his territory running at 50 percent of objective at the time Bill was hired.

When you discussed the territory with Bill and had a chance to analyze the information he gave you, you found the following:

Objective		$900,000
Accounted for		
Renewable contracts		
Trans Electro	$390,000	
Lyne Controls	25,000	
Central Instruments	35,000	
Tec-Trol	20,000	
Sensor Company	45,000	
Miscellaneous	100,000	
Current negotiations	000	
	$615,000	− 615,000
"Gap"		$ 285,000

Here is a territory with a 32 percent "gap"—large in itself, but more shaky in that one single account (Trans Electro) represents another 43 percent. Against this stands a relatively untried sales-man with only a basic knowledge of his territory. Regardless of Bill's experience in his selling or in his current territory, you want to work with him in terms of his objectives—his quota—and his "gap.")

(A mistake new managers tend to fall into lies in their uncon-sciously treating all of their salespeople as equals when it comes to measuring the way each covers his or her respective territory. I do not mean in terms of dollar quotas or targets but in setting objec-tives for them in terms of how they approach those territories, how they identify and work on closing the "gap.")

Back to Bill. With only a small group of existing accounts to maintain and no ongoing sales negotiations, his primary job will be twofold and simple: (1) to get around the territory and meet existing buyers—to identify who is buying what and from whom; (2) to pick specific targets. How Bill is going to determine which negotiations to go after to fill his "gap" will be determined by what he uncovers in this first attempt at identifying what his territory contains. Anything less and you have a salesman out there spinning his wheels, visiting friends, and putting in time—but not selling!

Introducing George Cassady

George was hired approximately two years previously. His sales experience consisted of selling welding kits used by some han-dicrafters and sold through hardware stores in rural areas. Al-though this prior experience did not meet the basic requirements for your firm, he was hired by your predecessor on the basis of his having had some technical schooling and on the fact that his sales record had been above average.

The territory he was assigned already had a number of solid accounts, which meant he spent more of his time maintaining ex-isting accounts than developing new ones. This year, however, re-vised objectives and the loss of two of those major accounts through cutbacks in their design programs resulted in a substantial "gap." Since George had spent little time developing new business, the net result is that he is in the same situation as any new sales-man. His first job is to find out just what potential his territory holds before he can develop a specific strategy.

George started to call on potential customers, determining

who bought what, from whom, why they bought what they did, and in what volume. When this identifying project was finished, George was asked to pick out those targets where he felt he had the best chance of developing a successful sales strategy. Unfortunately, while George could readily identify what was there, he seemed to have a mental block when it came to facing up to any kind of entrenched competition. When he would uncover a customer buying from a competitor, he would just back off with some excuse or another such as, "They're already buying a cheaper brand," and no amount of urging or suggestions on the part of the sales manager seemed to change him or get him actively going after the business.

Before you can set objectives for your salespeople you have to find out what they have to work with, both in terms of the marketplace and personally.

Introducing Lisa Sullivan

Lisa was also a fairly new representative with your firm, having been hired some five years ago directly from college, where she had graduated with an engineering degree. Following a brief training period at the factory, she had been assigned to her present territory.

An analysis of Lisa's territory revealed the following situation:

Objective	$750,000
Accounted for	
Renewable contracts	
D&A Enterprises	$180,000
Penright Company	105,000
BAB, Inc.	95,000
ABCO	130,000
Miscellaneous	40,000
Current negotiations	
Best Controls ($100,000 × 70 percent chance)	70,000

Electro-Metric
($80,000 × 90
percent chance)   72,000

Eator East
($60,000 × 60
percent chance)   36,000

Bower Contracting
($110,000 × 50 percent
chance)   55,000

IBM Corp.
($100,000 × 75   75,000
percent chance) $858,000   − 858,000

"Gap"   ($108,000)

In other words, there is a negative "gap" situation in this territory—a very favorable set of territory circumstances that presents an entirely different strategy position for you to consider.

Since this was a relatively undeveloped territory when Lisa was first assigned to it, you have a situation where she has developed a solid relationship with each of her accounts in order to be in this current position. Instead of a strategy based on prospecting to close the "gap," you will need five different strategies to maintain or increase position in each of the specific current negotiations. We will examine some strategy plans in a later chapter.

The Manager Creates the Salesperson's World

Any newly appointed sales manager, inexperienced or not as a manager, has the option of determining the type of environment in which the sales force will find their motivation. As a matter of fact, it is more than an option. Every manager establishes that environment either consciously or unconsciously, positively or negatively, actively or passively.

Every sales manager understands instinctively that an important function of the job revolves about the need to motivate the sales force. Unfortunately, this is also a fallacy, since we cannot motivate anyone any more than a salesperson can motivate a purchaser. People, psychological theory tells us, do things for their reasons, not ours. Thus, we can motivate no one. But we can, and do, create the environment in which motivation takes place—in which people (our employees, our sales force, our customers) motivate themselves. And depending on the nature of that environment, whether positive or negative, our employees will find positive or negative motivation.

I am certain you realize there is a lot more to it than this, but the basics are all there. We will have a chance to develop this more completely in a later chapter. For now, accept the fact that how you decide to set up the individual objectives, strategies, and tactics for each of your salespeople will have a powerful and lasting impact on their selling success.

You're setting up for your own success, too! For never forget, it is also your world you are creating, and this is why your superiors, perhaps without being able to put it into words, chose you because of your experience, past sales success, and potential ability to get from your sales force the very best they have to give. To do this, you have to develop in them the desire to achieve. Study after study points out people's desire for self-actualization, if someone would only show them how. That is motivation. That comes from what is around them—the environment in which they work—the world created by the sales manager. This is what being a manager is all about. How well you will succeed at it will depend on how well prepared you are for that success.

How do you get the training you need? You have already taken the first step with this book. Let the experience of other managers help you. Thus, you begin by doing exactly what we have been discussing. First, you set individual goals that aim each of your salespeople in his own needed direction, based on each one's different experiences and abilities. This goal direction also gives you the feedback you require to get a grasp on where your own needs lie. You must know where to find the opportunities and the threats presented by the external environment of your industry and the geography of the sales area you are responsible for. You want to know what strengths and weaknesses you have to work with.

Second, be open to what you find. Nothing you face as a sales manager will be completely foreign to what you faced in your sales role. The difference is that you now have to look at the world through the eyes and experiences of each individual salesperson you are responsible for directing, guiding, and developing. The strengths of each are different. The weaknesses of each are different.

Be open to your own growth through those you work with. Never stop learning. Read, listen, and communicate with your superiors. They know you are new at the game. If you are honest about your fears and about the direction in which you think you should go, they will help you. It is to their own advantage to do so. After all, they picked you. The last thing they want is your failure. But you have to be willing to meet them halfway. This entire area of people motivation is so important that we will discuss the details of how to make it work for you in the chapters to come.

Playing the Hand You're Dealt!

One final thought. You have inherited the sales force you have to work with. When you start, you seldom have much chance to pick your cards. You have to play the hand that's dealt, but that doesn't mean you cannot draw for a better hand after you have had the chance to study the game you are in and know what you are drawing to.

Using the "gap" approach I outlined earlier gives you a chance to study the instinctive selling ability of each of your salespeople. At this early stage in your career, you are probably feeling unsure of your own reactions to those abilities. With more experience, you will be able to categorize the selling instinct of all your salespeople within a few days of working with each of them. It is a matter of knowing what to look for.

Sam was employed as a salesman for an electrical components manufacturer. Although he had been selling in his particular territory for almost two years, when presented with the "gap" approach following a training program, it became evident that he had no idea where new business was going to come from. In other words, Sam would completely miss his targets unless his existing accounts somehow miraculously increased their purchases or serendipity uncovered new business during the year. Sam's manager gave him the immediate objective of identifying who in his territory was buying what, and from whom, exactly as if Sam were brand new. Unfortunately, although he could do a satisfactory job of maintaining existing accounts, Sam could not, even with specific direction, grasp the need for developing a plan of action for new business. Selling situations are not the same throughout industry. Sam might have been extremely competent in maintaining a solid list of existing customers, but faced with the need to get out and develop new business, Sam was in the wrong job.

When you find you have a salesman who just does not add to your goals, you do not have much choice—except to consider terminating or transferring him. One of the biggest fallacies of sales management is the feeling that "at least someone's covering the bases and maybe things will get better." It's a slowly eroding situation that will be a no-win game if you play it that way. This certainly does not mean you don't try to improve things. What it does mean is that you do not kid yourself that you personally are going to create a miracle. A boss from my past once said to me, "Dave, you can't polish what can't hold a shine." (Actually, his exact words were more colorful, but I think you get the idea.)

The point is, the success of your sales force is your responsibility. If some of them will succeed with no direct contribution, direction, training, or whatever from you—let them alone; you cannot improve on that. However, to the degree that you can add to their effectiveness, then you have the obligation—to them, to the company you both work for, and to yourself—to contribute to that increase in effectiveness to the degree of your capability. If nothing you do brings their effectiveness up to an acceptable point and within an acceptable time limit, seldom will more time improve the situation.

I hope these thoughts diminish rather than add to the confusion. Following the ideas presented in this first chapter will give you the foundation on which everything to be covered in the succeeding chapters will build in detail.

As happens so often in selling, and in life itself, the concepts are simple, straightforward, and easy to get down. The doing gets difficult because you are dealing with people, and people are very complex.

Set your goals and go after these goals step by step. Because you are dealing with people, the specific actions you take to reach those goals not only can become complex indeed but will be different in each situation you will face in your chosen career field.

Stay with it. Keep after those goals. Don't become impatient with the seemingly endless struggle for little progress. Sometimes it appears that we all chase the ever elusive gold at the end of the rainbow. Chase that gold. Someday you just might seize it!

2

Staffing Up: How Do I Get What I Need?

Concerned about filling your current opening for a sales position and making the correct choice? I know few sales managers who have not felt the same way. And many of the sales managers I know have been hiring salespeople for years.

Certainly the process is not to be taken lightly. It represents a serious commitment on the part of both the job candidate and the company. Yet few managers are truly trained or otherwise prepared for the task.

The selection process can involve a number of different issues, and I will attempt to cover each of the pertinent areas in this chapter. Thus we will begin with an in-depth look at the selection interview itself, which I will present in some detail. Later in the chapter I will try to bring the examples to life by telling you what was really involved in the final choices. I'll wind up with a look at some important "don'ts" and answer a number of questions that are repeatedly asked in seminars that I have conducted on the subject of selection.

The Selection Interview

The selection interview is the point at which all the information obtained from the application form, the résumé, and perhaps a preliminary telephone interview are integrated with other factors of the candidate's background that are relevant to the hiring decision. The interview serves two purposes. First, it determines the relevance of the candidate's work, educational, and personal background to the demands of the job. Second, it answers the candidate's questions about the company and the job itself. Selection is always a two-way street.

The selection interview should follow a logical sequence, but it should not be at all mechanical. Within each interview area, you should encourage the candidate to tell his or her own story. The less talking you have to do to maintain this pattern, the more successful the interview is likely to be. You should do only 10 percent to 15 percent of the talking and permit the candidate to take center stage. This enables you to sit back and analyze the significance of the applicant's remarks.

Let's stop here! If there is any single failure point in the employment interview process, it arises right here—early in the process. It is the net result of two misconceptions on the part of the interviewing manager. First, you are nervous simply because you know how important a proper choice is. Second, you want to present yourself and your company in the best light, just in case the candidate turns out to be someone you want to hire. So you do what is easiest for you: You start talking, which means you start selling. That means you are not listening. It means you have center stage. You give, but you don't get.

The key to a successful selection interview is based on the assumption that what the candidate has done in the past is the best indication of what he will do in the future. The résumé has given you a rough idea of the candidate's experience level. The interview is the process by which you will build on that sketchy résumé information and hopefully get enough data on which to base a hiring decision.

Interview Error No. 1: Not Knowing What to Look For

"Know what you are looking for!" Such an elementary statement! Why would we otherwise be bringing these potential salespeople into the interview? Well, then, let me ask you a question right now. If in the next minute, a candidate were to walk into your office to be interviewed for a sales position—what would you look for? And if you are really being honest with yourself right now, then you can see the problem. Namely, you don't know.

Now, I am assuming you have a job or position specification. Perhaps it's something rather formal prepared by your personnel department. Perhaps you filled out a form yourself. Look at it. What does it tell you? If it is at all similar to most position descriptions, it will not do much more than outline the most basic parameters of the job, the minimum requirements. Actually, most position descriptions are no more than the guidelines you used when skimming through the résumés you received—the guidelines that allowed you to make a preliminary decision on whom to talk to further. They presented the minimum requirements and got the candidates to the interview stage.

The following, then, is a summary of requirements from a typical position description. In looking at these, let's also make some assumptions about the company, the industry, and the product line you are hiring a salesman to handle.

Selecting the Candidates. Case study: The Acme Company. You are a new district manager for this manufacturer of electrical components, which are sold directly to major OEM (original equipment manufacturer) markets, primarily control panel builders, and through secondary distribution for the replacement market. Your salespeople are required to seek out and develop new OEM customers through their prospecting and following up leads, as well as work with the salespeople of selected electrical distributors in their training and in the sale of these units.

A review of the position description indicates the following basic requirements:

- That the prospective candidate have either an electrical engineering degree or a general business degree plus some technical training of an electrical or electronic nature.
- That the candidate have at least two years' experience selling electrical components in the OEM marketplace or through an industrial distributor.

In Figures 1 through 6 are reproduced résumés submitted in response to your newspaper inquiry. In reality, these are actual résumés submitted for positions similar to that described, although

(text continues on p. 33)

Figure 1. Résumé of Arthur Magnason.

Arthur Magnason

Experience:

1978 to present

Employed at Control Processes, Inc.
Manufacturer's rep for five years representing major industrial control process
equipment manufacturers.

Experienced in application and sales of
electrical components and control as-
semblies to OEM engineers directly and
to users through industrial electrical
supply houses.

Dealt with individual and multiunit
specifications, ranging between $1,500
and $1,500,000. (Partial customer list
attached.)

Education:

B.S., Electrical Technology, 1978.
MBA, Business (night school), 1981.

Personal data:

Married—no children.
Health: excellent.
Height: 5' 11".
Age: 27.

Figure 2. Résumé of Glen Greenwood.

Glen Greenwood

General:

 B.S., Industrial Management, 1981.
 Associate degree, Electrical Engineering,
 1979.
 Scholarship, State Realtors Board, 1977.
 Married—no children.

Work experience:
3/82 to present

 Sales Engineer, Corinth Coil Company.
 Responsibilities include initial customer
 contact, continuing follow-up with buyers,
 and application engineering for a line of
 speciality coils and transformers.

1/81 to 3/82

 Sales Trainee, W. S. Machinery Company,
 Industrial Division. Training involved
 both technical and selling skills and
 included the design, operation, and
 assembly of CNC machine tool controls,
 technical writing, and field sales
 experience for placement as a sales
 engineer.

8/80 to 3/81

 Research Assistant, School of History,
 Research assistant for various profes-
 sors at the university.

7/78 to 8/80

 Auto Mechanic, J&W Dodge. Full- and
 part-time work to pay for education.

Figure 3. Résumé of Robert Keen.

Robert Keen

Work experience:

1/80 to present	<u>Signal Systems Company, Sales</u> <u>Engineer</u>

Responsible for sales and marketing of services in design, engineering, and manufacturing of custom electronic test equipment to the industrial user market. Reported directly to the president and was responsible for forecasting and directing account/resource mix to achieve territory goals, with emphasis on direct sales handling of accounts. Also responsible for maintenance of operation schedules to assure timely delivery to accounts.

3/78 to 1/80	<u>B&W Sales, Inc., Manufacturer's</u> <u>Representative</u>

Responsible for the sales and marketing of electronic and electromechanical components to major OEM manufacturers. Reported directly to president. Formulated and implemented sales and marketing forecasts, plans, and presentations and conducted sales seminars and meetings for staff and customers.

8/77 to 3/78	<u>Burroughs Corporation, Senior Buyer</u> Responsible for procurement of electrical and electronic components.

<u>General</u>: B.S., Biology and Chemistry; MBA, Economics.

Born: June 8, 1951.   Wt: 175 lbs.

Married--4 dependents.

Figure 4. Résumé of Betty Dallens.

Betty Dallens

EDUCATION: B.S., Marketing, 1982.

MBA (current study—part-time).

WORK EXPERIENCE:

7/82 to present   <u>Sales Representative</u>, selling electronic components for area's largest independent distributor to engineering, maintenance, and purchasing departments. Responsibilities include expanding sales volume through a network of new and established accounts. Increased sales 40 percent in first year while surpassing quota each month. Accomplished highest monthly sales average in history of territory.

8/79 to 7/82   <u>Sales Representative</u>, Central Supply Company. Sales to physicians for manufacturer of medical instruments. Responsibilities included prospecting, making sales presentations, closing sales, and servicing accounts.

GENERAL: Part-time tennis pro at area's most successful club.

Instructor in electronics at local college.

Single; will relocate.

Figure 5. Résumé of Richard White.

Richard White

Work experience:

1979   Sales Engineer,
to   Breakstone Manufacturing Company.
date   - Responsible for sales and
                    service to heating element and
                    control customers.
                  - Reorganized territory to in-
                    crease sales 55 percent over
                    last year.
                  - Initiated new business with new
                    accounts while maintaining cur-
                    rent customers (list attached).
                  - Organized and conducted custo-
                    mer training program.

1977   Inside Sales,
to   Breakstone Manufacturing Company.
1979   - Responsible for assisting
                    national distributor network.

Education: B.S.E.E., with a minor in
              marketing and psychology.
              Wt.: 170 lbs.; ht.: 6'.
              Married--will relocate.

Figure 6. Résumé of Linda Maxwell.

Dear _____ :

For the past eight years, I have been successfully engaged in building my career in the technical sales area. In
just one year, I have increased the department's sales by
25 percent and broadened my account base by 50 percent.

My background--in service with an international construction equipment company and as a sales engineer with the leader
in diesel injection pumps and electrical equipment and, more
recently, in computer sales and technical application of
software with a newly formed numerical control computer
graphics firm--has given me a broad range of experience in
marketing technical products.

Some of my career accomplishments include:

Major Account Manager. In addition to selling electrical
products such as starters, alternators, motors, and switches,
I have successfully managed 14 accounts (7 made through my own
efforts). This position also included successful selling,
discussing technical information and establishing a testing
program with the OEM engineering staff, negotiating prices,
and coordinating delivery.

Marketing. I was required to forecast present and future
sales by quarter. Through my own market research, I defined
new markets for existing electrical products and developed a
product plan.

Technical Training. I effectively presented more than
30 dealer sales institutes, including hands-on application
training.

I have a B.S. in Marketing from the state university.

Sincerely,

Linda Maxwell

Linda Maxwell

the names of the candidates have been changed and some of the less pertinent detail has been omitted. All of the six were among those ultimately interviewed, and the results we will be discussing will be based on actual data. As a matter of fact, three of the six were eventually hired by one or another of the firms in this composite. The six résumés were chosen from the hiring activities of several different, but industry-related, companies. They reflect only a few of the many interviews conducted, but I believe they are a representative enough cross section that they can be used as examples in this case study. In reading these résumés, choose which of these individuals you regard as sufficiently suitable to call in for a selection interview.

In a moment, we will briefly analyze each of the six candidates. But before we do, let's see how we can eliminate or reduce major error No. 1. It is not enough just to look for "someone who can sell." Since past performance is the best indicator of future performance, you want to explore the area of each candidate's past performance. However, you do not consider past performance on the basis of a single deciding factor, such as work history, but from the standpoint of the candidate as a whole person. Thus, you have to be prepared to explore all pertinent areas of his or her background—work experience, education, training, and even social adjustment. The more relevant information that you can obtain about the applicant, the better basis you will have for making an intelligent selection decision.

What a Résumé Tells You. At this point in the selection process, you have accomplished one step. You have compared the résumé data with the specifics of what you are searching for. Admittedly, this will be sketchy. We are not interested here in what makes a good or bad résumé. Most, as you will have noted from those included herein, contain superfluous information. Some present barely enough; some engage in overkill. Be that as it may, what you have is what you will have to use for the purpose of elimination rather than for making a selection.

What *doesn't* a résumé tell you? It does not indicate whether an applicant can sell, will fit into your sales force personally, or is honest or hardworking or even intelligent. It *does not* tell you more things than it does tell you. But you have to start somewhere.

What the résumé (hopefully, at least) does tell you is how

closely the applicant's background just might fit. It should give you some idea of educational level. Does this fit with what you need? Where are this person's educational strengths and possible weaknesses in meeting your job requirements? What work experience might make up for an educational weakness?

What continuity is there in the work experience? Is this a job jumper? Maybe there are extenuating and logical reasons for the changes. Chances are the résumé will not tell you. You may want to go ahead with the interview to find out. If the résumé presents too many "holes," you might want to consider a telephone interview before bringing the person in for a face-to-face talk. How does the mental picture you get from the résumé in terms of apparent age, education, and experience—and your impression of the applicant as a person—mesh with your job needs?

Preparing to Meet the Applicant. All of the sample résumés on the previous pages meet, to some acceptable degree, the job requirements established. Therefore, the next step is to contact each of the applicants and arrange a time for a personal meeting.

- *Rule No. 1.* Within a short time of completing an interview, you will not accurately remember the key strengths or weaknesses of an applicant. This is particularly true when you are faced with the job of meeting a number of applicants.
  Recommendation: Take notes.
- *Rule No. 2.* If you do not know exactly what strength or weakness areas you are probing for, you cannot effectively conduct an interview.
  Recommendation: Develop a list of job criteria and have that list in front of you as a reminder during the interview. If you combine the two recommendations, you can make notes on your list to aid you in staying on the track.

What are "job criteria"? You tell me! What knowledge, skills, attitude, and behavior make an effective sales applicant for the job you are going to fill? For example, are you looking for conformity? Reliability? Loyalty?

Shown below is my own list of job criteria, developed over years of working with, training, and studying industrial salespeople. I do not claim that this is all there is or even that this is necessarily the best list. It works for me, and that is what is important about any list. I have developed it after considerable study, thought, and trial and error. Use it if you like. Modify it or change it, but begin to develop a list of job criteria that is yours.

1. *Interpersonal skills.* The ability to hold a directed and meaningful conversation. It involves listening to the other person, responding, getting an idea across.

     Key points to observe: How do the applicants handle the give-and-take of the interview? They should be selling themselves; do they? How do they go about getting their strengths across to you?

2. *Selling skills.* The skills of prospecting, negotiating, situational strategy development, and so forth. Does the candidate understand the "process of selling"—not necessarily from formal training, but instinctively?

     Key points: Does the applicant's current job demand prospecting, negotiating, and so on? What examples can the applicants offer to illustrate their approach to these areas?

3. *Territory control.* Reporting and analyzing territory and accounts.

     Key points: Do the applicants accept paperwork as an important part of the job or as a necessary evil? How well will they structure a "planned attack" on their new territory based on their past approach to territory management?

4. *Working with distributors.*

     Key points: What experience have they had in this area? How structured were past associations, or did they only occasionally "drop in" for coffee and conversation?

5. *Drive and reliability.*

     Key points: Are these applicants self-starters, or will they wait around for you to explain what to do next? Will they follow through? What will their customers say about them six months from now? What do their present customers say about them?

6. *Technical sales ability.*

     Key points: Is the knowledge the applicants display about their present line in tune with their experience? How has the applicant been "product-educated" in the past? If you do not offer an in-depth training program, how capable will this person be in acquiring what is necessary in terms of product knowledge?

All of these criteria should be evident from one of the four basic background areas each applicant brings with him or her: (1) early years, (2) educational years, (3) work years, (4) current years.

- *Rule No. 3.* A good selection is based on the statement that "what a person has done in the past, he will do in the future."

Your job is to probe the applicant's background areas using questions, situations, and discussion to give you sufficient insight regarding the job criteria to enable you to make the best selection decision. That is the key to eliminating error No. 1: Know what you are looking for.

Interview Error No. 2: The Unsupported Hunch and the Halo Effect

These two associated interviewing errors—the unsupported hunch and the halo effect—have a tendency to creep into the interviewing process of even the most experienced sales manager and prevent the interviewer from getting a realistic view of the candidate. In my own experience, I find they are a result either of not taking the time to prepare for the interview or of allowing myself to be mentally rushed during the session.

The Unsupported Hunch. The pressure of having to see a number of people in too short a time often leads interviewers to rely upon so-called hunches and jump to conclusions that have little or no basis in fact. Many of us, for example, have a tendency to classify people according to physical appearance or believe that if a particular characteristic comes to light, certain others will necessarily follow.

I recall that during an interview, a candidate made a statement that I considered not only wrong but ill-conceived on the part of a supposedly experienced salesman. My immediate reaction was that this individual was not going to be suitable. However, when I pushed my hunch aside and probed further, it turned out he had misunderstood my initial question.

The Halo Effect.   There is also a very human tendency to permit a single prominent characteristic to overshadow all others. Thus, you may be so favorably impressed with a candidate for one reason or another that you tend to rate him higher than he should be rated on other background traits. "He must be good. We both went to the same school!"

I had been interviewing all day, and by the time the last applicant arrived, I was feeling discouraged, in that none of the previous candidates had presented any clearly outstanding potential. When the last candidate walked into the room, his enthusiasm and good-natured personality were infectious, and I found myself actively noting little things that put him in a positive light while tending to discount otherwise negative statements and situations as insignificant. In other words, I wanted him to win.

The halo effect can also operate in the opposite sense. You are not being fair to the candidate if you permit one shortcoming to influence your judgment disproportionately regarding his other traits. The key to dealing with an apparent weakness is to determine whether you could help overcome the shortcoming if you were this person's manager.

Some initial impressions are very valuable to you as an interviewer, but only if you are able to support them by obtaining corroborating information. You may see that a given candidate appears strongly aggressive, for example. This gives you a signal to search for aggressiveness in other areas. On the other hand, such initial aggressiveness may prove to be a sign of tactlessness. Again, you must use such a first impression only as a clue on which to base further research.

Beginning the Interview

To gain the candidate's complete confidence and establish appropriate rapport, the interview must be conducted in private. But privacy entails more than four walls. The word implies lack of interruption of any kind. When conducting an interview in your office, it seems a simple courtesy to cut off all telephone calls and present a closed door to the rest of the world or otherwise discourage others in the organization from barging in.

Since a good percentage of sales interviews are held in the field away from the office, a hotel setting can make a suitable place with a little forethought. If a full day's interview schedule is in the offing, I would suggest that serious consideration be given to engaging a small suite. Even with careful budgeting constraints, this should not present a hardship. A "studio" room is available in most hotels for little more than the price of a regular sleeping room, and most hotels have reasonably priced "display rooms" that can be fitted with a table and chairs, given any reasonable notice.

What should be avoided under almost all circumstances is an interview in a public place, either a hotel lobby or—the latest fad—crammed into the corner of an airline clubroom. I have observed (and listened in on) too many such interviews. As an objective observer, I cannot recall a single one that presented a relaxed candidate. Furthermore, although the applicant may not be in a position to make a public display of his feelings, the individual cannot but be less than impressed with being subjected to such an interview. One of the most uncomfortable situations for a salesperson is to be put in the position of making a sales presentation to a buyer in a lobby with others looking on. Yet sales managers (mostly ex-salesmen) appear to subject sales applicants to the same treatment they would abhor. It is just not professional.

Even under the best of conditions, interruptions do occur and make the interviewer's job more difficult. If you take a telephone call, for example, the applicant will have a chance to think back over the previous discussion. The applicant may conclude that he has given too much information about personal or professional shortcomings. As a result, when the interview resumes, he may try to prevent you from finding out more information. An interruption of any kind not only sidetracks the interviewer's train of thought but stops the process of free-flowing analysis.

The first few minutes of any interview can be critical, but I suspect for the wrong reasons if you accept the rationale given in the textbooks. This time period is critical, they state, to establish rapport, to make the applicant feel at ease. I do not disagree, but I think these first minutes are also important for another reason.

First impressions in a selling situation are important. How does the applicant handle making a first impression? While setting the stage is also important, do not become so involved with the preliminaries that you are not critically aware of your candidate's behavior from the first moment.

Once the applicant has been greeted appropriately and seated comfortably, small talk can be used to encourage him to do most of the talking, even at this early stage. The sound of the candidate's own voice will give him confidence, ease initial tension, and help break the ice. If the applicant is not immediately put on the spot by being asked for the particulars of his background, he should not feel the need to hold back with quite the normal defensive reaction you would expect. After all, you can be "Mr. Nice Guy" and still know what it is you are searching for. As a matter of fact, it is easier.

Presented below is the beginning of an interview with Art Magnason, one of the applicants whose résumé you have reviewed. It will illustrate many of the elements of a good interview that we have been discussing.

SM (sales manager): Art Magnason? Come on in.

Art: [Quietly but pleasantly] Yes. You're Mr. Smith?

SM: Yes, Ed Smith. [I offer my full name and let it go at that. I want to see how quickly the applicant gets onto a first-name basis. Too quickly and I might probe further for aggressiveness. If we don't get there at all, I might question whether there is any aggression.] Put your coat over there. [He seemed unsure of himself, perhaps just nervous.] Did you have any trouble finding us?

Art: No, not at all. A number of my present customers are in the area.

SM: Oh, who are they?

Art: Imperial Electronics. I'm quite proud of that one. I've had all their business now for two years. [Score a point for interpersonal relations: He has told me quite nicely he worked hard for "that one." I notice the nervousness has disappeared and he is in control. I'll cut the introductory period short and begin a directed interview rather than just seeing where he takes me. I find that when I maintain control of the subject area, I have an easier time keeping track of the criteria I am probing for.]

SM: As you are aware, we are searching for a salesman in this area. This is only a preliminary meeting to see how well we fit each other. I'm here to listen to you, and then I want you to know all about us and what we are trying to accomplish in this territory. [I have set the stage, outlining the interview process and how we will proceed.] You're currently with Control Processes? [A direct question, but it brings up the topic of work experience and it prevents an assumption that is easy to make—note the answer.]

Art: No, I left them last month. [He pauses; so do I. I decide to just wait him out.] We had quite a shake-up when Mr. Clemson, the owner, died. His son took over, and . . . well, we never did get along.

SM: That's rough, but it happens all the time. [Reinforcing that there is nothing to worry about, and he can say anything he wants.] How big is the firm?

Art: Five of us plus a secretary.

SM: What have you enjoyed most about your experiences there?

And so the interview goes. It is a process of moving through the background areas of each of the applicants with probing questions and discussion to determine how each measures up in light of the job criteria you have chosen as your measure.

Is there a specific order to follow in probing background areas? No, a lot will depend on how the interview shapes up during the opening phase. Normally, work experience is the easiest area to get into, since the applicant knows this is an area you are going to discuss.

If the candidate has not been out of school too long or has only recently graduated, you might find it easier to start with educational background years. I find that it is easier to bring early development and current life backgrounds into the discussion during more relaxed moments of the interview. However, if I feel I am lacking information regarding one or more of the job criteria and I cannot pin it down through the applicant's educational or work experiences, I will make an effort to concentrate on either early or current life situations, depending on the applicant's age, openness to discussion, and just a "feeling" about which of the areas might be a more appropriate route. The background areas are not a requisite, only a means of filling in what I want to know to determine how well the applicant meets the job criteria.

Experience shows, however, that the best results will come from not having to "jump around"—that is, move from one area to another to develop your information. On the other hand, you may seldom find job criteria data coming from one particular area of probing versus another. The key here is to know what you are looking for and be open to any clues that you can then follow up. That is another reason for having a written outline of background areas and job criteria to keep you on track.

Figure 7 presents one idea of how such a worksheet could be constructed. It does not necessarily have to be in printed form or carefully ruled in blocks. Such a matrix can be roughly drawn on a pad and be just as effectively used.

How do you develop the kinds of questions leading to discussion that gets to the criteria? Some suggestions are given below.

To probe selling skills:

- "How did you find new accounts?" or "Was that something that just seemed to come along?" (Whatever the answer, it

Figure 7. Format of a job criteria worksheet.

Job criteria	Work	Education	From life
1. Interpersonal skills			
2. Selling skills			
3. Territory control			
4. Distributors			
5. Drive/reliability			
6. Technical			

gives you a direction in which to proceed further. By asking such a dual-directed question, it does not put any emphasis on one area as being more important than another. *Rule:* Never show displeasure at any reply.)

- "I recall when I was selling to a Detroit firm" (or Cleveland or wherever), "I found dealing with those automotive buyers" (or steel or major component buyers or whatever) "really made my life tough! Did you find it different in this area?"
- "How would your present boss say you handled that part of your job?"
- "Our salespeople find it difficult getting distributor salesmen to make joint calls. Does your present company experience a similar problem?" (Such a question is also used to probe the "working with distributors" area. Note the use of "your company" to make the reply less personal; yet experience shows that in 97 percent of such replies, the response is a personal one.)

To probe drive and reliability:

- "You mentioned your success at closing that last order. I gather that was a long time coming. Did you have a specific strategy to follow?" "What happened that made you feel you were going to get that one?" (Also a lead-in to other criteria.)
- "When did you decide to get into sales as a career?" "Was there someone in your past who influenced you in your choice of a selling career?"
- "What experience have you had with selling to shop maintenance people?" "How about dealing with an entrenched competitor?" "What was your strategy to meet this situation?"
- "What words would your best (worst) customer use to describe you as a salesman? Why?"

Note, in all of the above, how readily any reply can take you into any of the criteria areas. As a matter of fact, the secret does not lie in the questions themselves but in the use of questions to open discussion. The more the applicants are directed and encouraged to talk freely about their experiences, the more effective the interview will be.

All of these probing questions will fall into one of four general categories:

1. *Situational questions,* in which the interviewer presents a situation and asks the applicants how they would respond to or handle that situation.
2. *Comparison questions,* in which the applicants are asked to compare their experience with the one proposed.
3. *Self-evaluation,* in which the applicant is asked to express his or her feelings or emotions about the situation presented by the interviewer.
4. *Shockers!* A special category to probe the applicants' ability to handle stress. For example:

    "Why would you want this position?"

    "Somehow I get the impression you are rather weak in _____" or "Somehow I get the feeling you are putting too much effort and time on _____as opposed to _____."

    "What kind of a selling style do you have?" "Is this any good? Why?"

Finally, remember that no interview should be a final one unless you are sure you have the answers you need to make the very best decision. The lack of any information you feel may be pertinent always justifies one more review with a final candidate. Given a choice, I would prefer a breakfast/lunch/dinner interview, since the more relaxed environment is always more conducive to an extended discussion regarding the more emotional areas of an applicant's psychological makeup. Yet at times, a more formal follow-up interview may be necessary to probe areas needing explanation. This is a major decision—for both of you.

Making a Final Choice

Let's look at a summary of the interviewers' final comments on each of the six candidates whose résumés you reviewed earlier.

Note how little of the final decision was based on résumé information.

Art Magnason. Here's an applicant who interviewed very well, once he conquered his initial nervousness. However, he displayed a lack of both knowledge and interest regarding the interpersonal side of dealing with people and placed too much emphasis on the technical aspects of his product. While this might have been ideal for some product lines and in some industries, it was not felt to be favorable in the present hiring situation. Applicant rejected.

Glen Greenwood. The applicant handled himself very well throughout the interview. He displayed a quiet but direct approach to interpersonal relationships and appeared to adapt well to different buyer personalities, as expressed in discussion of different sales situations he has handled. Relating several experiences showed he does not hesitate to "bend" policy slightly to achieve an end but at the same time is conscious of being "out of line." Although inexperienced, he was quick to pick up on techniques suggested by the interviewer. His primary weakness is in the area of working with distribution, owing to lack of previous experience. The interviewer felt this could be overcome with counseling and training. Applicant hired.

Robert Keen. Discussion determined that the applicant is more marketing-oriented than sales-oriented. With probing, Keen admitted that he was actually fired from each of his sales jobs because his superiors "were too demanding," or did not give him "enough time to complete an assignment or develop the territory properly." Applicant rejected.

Betty Dallens. Applicant was self-assured and controlled the interview very effectively through her own use of questions. She had good technical grasp, apparently owing to her part-time work as a technical instructor. Her Central Supply Company position was part-time while attending college. Her current position holds no future in sales management since it is in a closely held family firm. The interviewer left the meeting with the feeling that the applicant was "too good to be true," and two additional interviews were arranged, one at breakfast and another at dinner. The applicant remained open and raised no further questions in the interviewer's mind. Applicant hired.

Richard White. The applicant displayed an irritating habit of breaking into a conversation before a question was completely presented. He did not carry the conversation but replied with a minimum of information as if unsure of the answer and waited for the interviewer to offer a new question. He then responded poorly to situational questions. Interview was cut short. Applicant rejected.

Linda Maxwell. The applicant was vivacious and enthusiastic, although interviewed late in the day. She displayed good interpersonal control and asked effective questions. Her technical background tends to be weak, although she has received good training from a previous employer. From the conversation, the applicant appears very thorough and has a good grasp of industrial processes and the instinctive selling skills necessary. She is organized, plans each job, and appears to be able to adapt her plans to the real world as she meets it. She has a basic lack of understanding of distribution but has had to deal with distributor personnel as a manufacturer's representative. Her major strength appears to be a willingness to take on difficult assignments and find a means to carry them out, as exemplified by the successes achieved on her present job. Her reasons for leaving previous positions were: An earlier position was terminated owing to department layoff as a result of low sales in the construction industry; a second position—with a small, undercapitalized firm—was not secure. She claims to be looking for a career move. She is married, and her husband is a computer specialist with a major firm located in this city. Applicant hired with some reservation, owing to her lack of technical expertise.

The reader should bear in mind that these are real situations, although details and names have been changed to protect the individuals' identities. In each case, the interviewer is making a judgment based on the perception of what criteria and behavior will be successful. Recall the feeling that the interviewer of Glen Greenwood expressed in discussing risk taking as a willingness to "bend" policy to achieve a result. To another interviewer, or in a different context or situation, this would have been unacceptable behavior. In other words, the selection process is an art, a skill—hardly a science. There is no secret to be learned, just as there are no "magic" questions, only an approach.

Some Things You Can't Do!

I do not think discrimination is intended by any manager, and avoiding such acts is not a major part of interviewing and selection skill. Nevertheless, no discussion of selection would be complete today without a reminder that there are a number of subject areas (seven, in fact) that are "off limits"—not only because they represent poor protocol but because the law says so.

Sex. We're not talking here about the "casting couch" kind, which is pretty obvious, but about any implication in the interview, advertisement, or notes you make to the effect that being female is not accepted or might present a problem. Just for a moment, turn back to the notes from the interview with Linda Maxwell and observe the reference to her being married and her husband's job—actually very innocent notes having no apparent bearing on the outcome of the interview. Unfortunately, in a contested hiring situation, courts might just find that such seemingly innocent notes implied she was "safe" to hire since her husband probably would not be transferred.

What are other danger areas? Possibly a discussion oriented toward "planning a family" or, for that matter, toward a spouse's transfer or career plans.

Recommendation: Do not see a "female" applicant. Instead see only a bundle of knowledge, skills, and attitudes as they relate to the job to be done. (And besides, some of the female industrial salesmen I have had working for me could sell rings around a great number of men.)

Other potential problem areas to be aware of include: race, religion, age, finances, criminal record, handicaps.

Recommendation: Use your common sense. Do the best job you can to find the most qualified person to fit the job criteria; keep the conversation directed toward the job requirements; and don't worry.

Some Final Thoughts

In closing this chapter, here are a number of questions that are asked over and over and that are just as surely on the mind of every new sales manager.

Most companies appear to have a rule that any sales candidate must be interviewed by two levels of management before being hired. Is this really necessary? I have to say yes for several reasons. As you have seen, selection is an art, a skill. Being human, even the best and most experienced can miss something important. The errors of hunch and the halo effect creep into the interviewing process when least expected. Perhaps more important, hiring is a serious commitment by any company. Having two or even more levels of management interview and concur also tells the applicant that the company does take this seriously.

With everyone worried about saying the wrong thing and getting sued, how worthwhile are reference checks? First, I really wonder if a reluctance to discuss an ex-employee is due totally to fear of a lawsuit or rather to the growing realization that an employee who "couldn't make it" in one environment or sales position might be more than acceptable in another firm or position. Be that as it may, you at least need to verify that applicants actually worked where and when they said they did. I once interviewed an outstanding candidate who lied about his entire work experience—and did it very successfully until we checked past employment. In addition, in a manager-to-manager discussion, you might be surprised at how much information can be contained in a refusal to discuss the performance of an ex-salesperson. On the positive side, I find that few managers hesitate to point out the good things about someone they have had in their employ. "Would you hire him again?" is still a good question, and its answer is always worth your careful attention.

What makes a good employment ad? An effective employment ad is one that gets the best possible candidate to respond to it. If you spend any time looking through the Sunday classified ads (and this is an excellent suggestion if you are thinking of placing an ad of your own—what strikes *you*?), you will quickly notice a number of things that separate the good from the mediocre. The following is a list of personal preferences, based on my own experience of what works best. It is included only as a guideline.

- Bold framing and large, separate headlines make an ad more forceful and dynamic—quicker to be picked out by someone just skimming.
- Tell the reader specifically what you are looking for. Do not beat around the bush. Everyone's eager, dynamic, loyal, brave, and true. After all, the objective is 2 or 3 outstanding applicants rather than the 300 who think they can sell anything.
- Unless there is a specific reason to avoid doing so, give the

name of the company and the product line or division. This also eliminates those who really do not fit (some of them, anyway).

- Unless you are searching in a narrow local market, your best bet will be the Sunday classified section under a "sales" classification. If you are searching in a town with more than one paper, I would suggest placing the ad in both. Salespeople with potential may subscribe to the other paper.

It is impossible in such a limited space to reach this point and be able to say, "That's all there is!" We have merely scratched the surface of a critical function of a manager's job. Hopefully, it will be enough to enable the new manager to approach the selection task with some confidence. As a boss of mine once said about the subject: "Whether you think you can or not, you must!"

3

Setting Objectives:
What Objectives Are
Meaningful?

You have spent time with each of your salespeople and have a fairly good idea of their territories. You have met the key buying influences, tried to give each of the salespeople some insight into your own personality and goals as a manager, and told them something about what is expected of them. More important, you have had the opportunity of watching them in action with their customers, in their selling approach, and in their approach to territory management.

As managers, we have a number of goals or objectives, all of which should direct us toward the greater objectives set for the entire corporation. They help us become better managers of business units or departments for which we are responsible. The individual members of the sales force also have objectives—quotas. Even so, they also need a number of lesser objectives to help them "manage" their sales territories. But that raises an interesting question. Are all salespeople responsible for managing a territorial unit, just as managers are responsible for a business unit? We will open the discussion of objectives by examining that question. Only then will we be in a position to begin developing meaningful objectives for the sales force. Finally, we will try to put the subject of budget-ing into proper perspective for the sales manager.

Territory Management: Myth or Necessity?

Territory management is no myth. There is nothing fanciful about it. It exists. To what degree it is alive and well may be another matter.

Every salesman is a territory manager, only because he must manage that territory to survive as a salesperson. As with the ques-tion "Do managers really manage?" (answer: "That is what they're paid to do!"), so we might also ask, "Do salesmen really manage their territories?" And the answer is also, "Yes. Because that is what they're paid to do!"

Given the nature of the job, a salesman spends more time out of sight and hearing of the manager than in direct contact. This means that even the salesman with the most strictly proscribed reg-imen is faced with the need for some amount of independent deci-sion making. The far greater majority of salesmen have quite a bit of freedom to adapt to the circumstances of their jobs. To meet these circumstances effectively, they are required to manage what goes on in their territories.

Who Gets Called on Next?

An old sales adage says, "If a salesman can cover all his territory, the territory is too small." Without any planning, that is undoubt-edly correct. The problem is not merely in planning, but in plan-ning for what? And how? Let's look at three basic approaches to territory planning and coverage.

First Approach: Cataloging the Customers by Importance

There are any variety of categories we could use to catalog customers by their importance. The idea is to segregate prospects and customers into a number of groups—for example: A, B, C, and possibly D. The A group may all be those with a potential sales volume of, say, $1 million or more. The B group would have a sales potential between $500,000 and $1 million; the C group between $200,000 and $500,000; and the D group anything over $10,000 and up to $200,000.

Next, a decision has to be made regarding the average number of calls to be scheduled on each category during some set period. For example:

A accounts—once each week
B accounts—twice monthly
C accounts—once a month
D accounts—every other month

Now there is nothing holy or cast-in-concrete about such call schedules. They are planning guidelines only. They tell the salesperson what ought to be done, all things being equal. Since nothing ever is equal from the minute it leaves the planning stage, I would daresay that any salesperson who was sticking religiously to a planned schedule either missed something in the planning or is missing something even more important in the selling. That is just the nature of things.

The next step is to plot the various customer categories on a map of the territory and begin the process of heuristically balancing the routes that will most advantageously develop the logistics of getting around the territory.

Incidentally, *heuristic balancing* (a term borrowed from production-line management) essentially is the process of balancing a parts-transportation route or stations on an assembly line by trial and error following some prescribed priority rules for establishing the process. We lay out sales routes in the same manner, by trial and error, the rules being the number of A or B calls per week or month, the average length of call, and of course, some implied knowledge of the specific customer involved, since, obviously, even a C-group customer with a "hot" sales negotiation is going to be getting more attention than another customer in the same class.

Second Approach: The Logistics of Travel

It is relatively easy to plan for working a territory such as Minnesota and Wisconsin when the majority of accounts will be located in major industrial areas and the rest will fall somewhere in between. Thus, we schedule one week in the Minneapolis area and the next in the Milwaukee area. One swing covers Madison and perhaps Janesville to the south; the next swing comes down through Appleton and perhaps Green Bay.

Regardless of the complexity of a territory, the planning begins with asking the salesperson to indicate in broad terms what the plans are to cover that territory.

> I begin every new position as a sales manager by asking each salesman to give me a map indicating the routes, or "legs," of his territory coverage by weekly time periods. For example, a salesman stationed in Detroit and covering Ohio, Michigan, and Indiana might break his weekly trips into five segments:

> Leg 1   Detroit and vicinity, with Toledo
> Leg 2   Western Michigan and northern Indiana
> Leg 3   Fort Wayne, Indianapolis, Lima
> Leg 4   Columbus and back through Canton
> Leg 5   Dayton, Cincinnati

The interesting thing about such an exercise is that precisely what is proposed, whether by a new salesman or someone experienced in the territory (and probably being asked to plan for the first time), is not really important. The point is that the salesman has to think through a plan, and the call reports will then reflect the plan in action. If they do not, then it is time to change the plan—to rethink what is being accomplished.

Once such a plan is implemented, it can be refined. In some instances, separate routes may be planned for subterritories. For example, a salesman covering the states of Illinois and Michigan may have several blocks or "legs" planned for covering the entire territory and smaller subroute plans for, say, Chicago or Milwaukee. Perhaps there may even be several subroutes planned for sections of Chicago.

Third Approach: A Combination

What should have become obvious by this time is that both of the previous approaches can be combined—and probably should be. I kept them separate to outline their concepts. Whether they are combined or not will be a decision based on the geography of the particular territory, the product sold, and the customer categories. For example, a product line sold to all types of industries would create a different logistics problem for sales-territory planning than one sold to, say, only machine-tool manufacturers. The sale of medical capital equipment to hospitals creates a different set of circumstances than the sale of blood-collecting and -analysis programs to physicians.

I would strongly recommend that any new manager coming into a sales management position begin by asking each salesperson to plan and provide such data for the following reasons:

- It gives you a springboard into further territory planning.
- It focuses on the time-management aspect of sales activity.
- It acts as a checkpoint in reviewing associated planning tools such as call reports and in developing of key-account strategies.
- It aids in answering the question, "How professional is this salesperson's approach to territory management?"

Let's Set Territory Objectives

If you think back to what was said in Chapter 1 about using the "gap" approach to ultimately set territory objectives, you will now see how this comes into the picture. You will recall that in identifying the "gap" in a territory, three basic elements came into play:

1. Known accounts whose business is expected to repeat with probably little more than continued attention and good service.
2. Known potential sales that are currently being developed by the salesperson.
3. An amount of business from unknown sources that has to be identified if the salesperson is going to meet the territory quota.

The approach that a salesperson will take in developing any or all of these three "gap" segments represents an initial set of strategic objectives. However, before we proceed any further, let's look at the nature of business objectives.

The Nature of Objectives

Not too long ago, I stayed in a hotel of a chain that advertised that "The entire purpose of this business is in its service to the customer." Now I am sure that a similar policy is in effect somewhere in the manuals or advertisements of just about every company doing business with the outside world. Yet what is the net result of such a policy the next time a delivery truck with such a company's name on the side cuts off another driver (perhaps the traffic manager for its biggest customer)? And so it is with every department store, bank, restaurant, or gas station whose employees forget the objectives of the business.

> I used to do business with a certain travel agency until I stood in the center of its office one day listening to a lengthy personal telephone conversation that was obviously more important to that firm than I was.

In both the long and the short run, it does not really matter what industry you are in. What matters is how you relate to the needs of each customer. The failure in each of the above examples did not lie in the sincerity of those businesses or in the firmness of their managements' desire to establish objectives, but in mistaking good intentions for objectives. Having satisfied customers, providing quick response, and giving customer service are intentions, not objectives.

Peter Drucker, the noted business writer and consultant, tells us, "The purpose of a business is to create a customer." This is the purpose, not the objective, of a business. Purposes are intentions, credos. Purpose creates environments and gives direction to the organization. Objectives, on the other hand, are specific. Objectives are end results. They establish the measure of the success of the business.

Objectives, of necessity, must be measurable. Thus stated, objectives are often financial or numerical. If you do not know what you want for an end result, you have no means of controlling how you will get there. Without having a measurable objective, there is no way to say, "This is under control!" or "This is out of control!" What cannot be counted or weighed cannot be measured. Unless you can evaluate a result by some scale, some standard, some parameter, you cannot control it.

One of management's most difficult moments in setting objectives on which to act comes in the attempt to establish objectives that are meaningful and relevant. It has been suggested that a possible test for developing specific objectives can be to ask three questions regarding each objective:

> Under what circumstances would you not want to meet this objective?
> Why do you want to meet this objective?
> If you failed to meet this objective, would your business (territory) fail?

It was further suggested that the only legitimate answers to those questions were, respectively, "None," "To survive," and "Yes." While such replies may appear unduly severe, they do effectively stress the main characteristics of relevant objectives.

> Joe Bates has the following objective for his sales territory: "To successfully obtain 60 percent of all active sales negotiations that close during the quarter."

Under what circumstances would Joe not want to meet this objective? Answer: "None!" Suppose as Joe's manager you can say, "We will not take any orders below our published sales prices." Does this imply a different answer than "None"? If so, perhaps we will have to rework the objective to read, "To obtain 40 percent of all negotiations," on the grounds that the additional 20 percent will primarily be price negotiations in which we will not enter. On the other hand, when the objective was originally set at 60 percent, this may have been taken into account. If so, the test has been met.

Why would your sales district want to meet this objective? Would the answer be, "To survive"? Would the territory fail if this objective were not met? Would the answer be, "Yes"? However, even if actual failure or survival itself are not at stake, if you substitute *meet quota* for *survive* and *fail*, then the objective would also meet these tests and can be regarded as relevant.

Any objective is dependent on a number of subgoals that must be accomplished if the primary objective of "meeting quota" is to be met. Thus, we have a fourth test to be applied: "Are the short-term results in balance with the longer-range objectives?" If management fails in the task of setting objectives, it is usually not in setting either long-term objectives or short-term objectives, but in balancing the short-term within the framework of the long-term. Five-year goals are not made in leaps, but in short steps. Annual targets are achieved in monthly and quarterly increments. It is as important for each salesperson's monthly or quarterly objectives to be tested in terms of their contribution to the annual quota as it is for the subgoals of the entire sales district to be tested in terms of their contribution to the goals of the division or the company.

In addition to balancing short-term objectives within the longer view, the manager has to continuously reevaluate the facts on which those objectives are based. All attempts at goal setting are adventures into the future, and thus into the unknown. To do what has to be done effectively, the decisions on which goals are based must be built on facts—even if, at times, this involves only a single fact.

The problem is, for really important decisions, you never seem to have enough facts, only assumptions. There is nothing wrong with assumptions. Managers live by them—and then unfortunately react to those assumptions as if they were facts. Assumptions are only valid until further data prove them invalid—then you make another assumption.

Suppose the objective is "To increase sales of product Z by 100 percent each quarter." This depends, among other things, on a continual questioning of both the ability and the motivation of the salesperson to achieve and the probability of external conditions' reacting favorably. There are few things that will distinguish competent from incompetent management quite so fast as an ability to balance objectives with reality.

Janet set the following objective for Fred, one of her salesmen: "To identify four new potential accounts each week through cold-call prospecting." By the end of the month, Fred was barely turning in three new accounts each week. Janet reviewed Fred's call reports and spent several days traveling with him. Finding no logical explanation for the results being turned in except in the possibility that the potential in Fred's territory was below the level assumed, Janet and Fred reestablished his goals at three new accounts each week.

Time showed that the initial assumptions had indeed been erroneous.

Setting Objectives

Ed Smith, the newest district manager for the company, has been reviewing the sales activity in the territory of Ron Harris, one of his salesmen. Ron has been in the territory some two years and has a number of potential sales under development, along with a good base of annual contracts that will be renewed shortly. In discussing the "gap" situation in Ron's territory, the following picture emerged:

Objective		$1,000,000
Accounted for		
Renewable contracts	$400,000	
Current negotiations	250,000	
Miscellaneous	150,000	
	$800,000	− 800,000
"Gap"		$200,000

After traveling with Ron, reading through his call-planning and key-account reports, and discussing the situation with him, Ed makes a number of assumptions:

Ron does not plan a strategy for a particular sales negotiation but tends to react from call to call. Ron needs to learn to read what is happening in a key sales situation and plan his moves.

Ron is not a good closer, preferring to let a sale run its course rather than push for a decision. Ron must learn to control the close of a key negotiation.

Ron does not do a sufficiently good job of uncovering new potential. He needs to achieve more directed prospecting.

Ron does not sell the "full line." Instead, he tends to let the customer pick what is planned without presenting any options. Ron needs to direct his sales effort, particularly toward product H, which is way behind quota.

On the basis of the above, Ed has prepared the following objectives for a discussion with Ron:

1. To develop specific strategy and tactics for all sales negotiations with a potential volume of $50,000 or more. (To be
   submitted for review and possible revision within three
   weeks.)
2. To successfully close 80 percent of all key sales negotiations
   scheduled to be completed during the current quarter.
3. To identify two new potential accounts each month
   through cold-call prospecting.
4. To increase sales of product H by 150 percent each month
   until sales are on target.

The specific words used in expressing each objective may vary
as new facts are uncovered. These objectives will be reviewed peri-
odically by Ed and added to or otherwise modified to meet changing conditions. They are based on Ron's specific need for improvement, which was triggered by the territory information that came
to light in the course of identifying the territory "gap."

Given Ed's current knowledge and understanding, does what
he has come up with meet the criteria for good objectives outlined
earlier? Let's check this. Under what circumstances would Ron not
want to meet these objectives? Answer: "None!" Why does Ron
want to meet these objectives? Answer: "To meet quota!" If Ron
failed to meet these objectives, would he fail to meet quota? Answer: "In all probability!" Do these objectives meet the long-range
district objectives? Answer: "Yes!"

This, then, introduces the essential elements of setting short-
term territory objectives. While objectives are specifically set for
areas that need improvement, they are seldom confined to just one
area. In Ron's situation, his manager established four objectives.
Nor are all objectives necessarily sales- or customer-oriented. Even
objectives directed toward personal improvement are valid, provided they meet the criteria we have established for good objectives.

What the Sales Manager
Needs to Know About Budgets

Any sales manager can produce a plan to penetrate 20 percent of
his territory or to capture a specific account. But those same sales
managers will probably fail to show you how they can stay within

their allotted expenses while doing so. The job of the manager is to bring all the elements of a territory together at one time to achieve all the objectives at a cost that produces a profit along with growth and remains within the bounds of not only the possible but the necessary. To achieve this, the sales manager needs to understand what a budget is all about.

As a new sales manager, you may have had little—or next to nothing—to say about the budget you have been handed for your district. If this is the case, you will have to deal with the budget you are stuck with. Yet understanding the process of budgeting is still necessary if you are to deal with it successfully. Let's listen to several top managers talk about their views on the subject:

- "The most important measure of a manager's skill is the manager's ability to maintain a budget—on schedule. I don't mean just in total, I mean on every detailed line; and I don't mean by the end of the fiscal year. I expect the manager to be on target every month."
- "A budget is not a caveat; it's a road map. Before I criticize a manager too strongly for going over budget, I want to know why. When a budget is missed—over or under—I'm more concerned with the reasons why. There may be very good reasons. This doesn't mean that we don't have to take immediate, and perhaps drastic, action to get back on budget, but that's being a manager. All the budget does is point out where the trouble spot is likely to be."
- "I think budgeting every item in detail is essential to good budgeting, but I'm more concerned with the total on the bottom line than with whether one or two items are out of phase. No manager can sit down 12 to 15 months previously and predict what's going to happen. If the manager can, his budget will only be made up of fixed costs—committed costs. More important is the person's managerial ability to keep balancing all the items over which he does have control in order to keep the bottom line on target."
- "I just can't talk about the importance of staying on budget without bringing in the bigger picture. Most managers have a target in the form of an annual budget. This is a delusion. It is not a target; it's a forecast. A target is what you want to happen; a forecast is what you expect to happen. No man-

ager can manage only one aspect of the job and be called successful."

Before commenting on these diverse views, let's take a look at the budget itself.

What Is a Budget?

Essentially, a budget is a forecast of costs for some period in the future. As a forecast, a budget is based on three assumptions:

- That past costs and income can be used to establish basic trends for the future.
- That expected future events will occur—that is, anticipated increases in the cost of labor or material, an increase in market penetration, or an increase in travel costs will happen as predicted.
- That the sequence of cost activity or outlay will occur evenly, at a monthly rate of $\frac{1}{12}$ the annual amount.

Overriding everything is a fourth assumption: that anyone can forecast the future. This may be possible, but can it be done accurately?

To understand the role played by the budget, we must see it in relation to the whole—where it fits with the other functions of management. In general, there are five basic functions performed by a manager:

1. Planning and setting objectives
2. Staffing and organizing
3. Supervising and controlling
4. Developing people
5. Measuring results

Within the framework of these five functions, every manager has two specific jobs:

- To develop synergism. This means, please God, to create a whole that is greater than the sum of its parts—to make the achievements of the district add up to more than the individual actions of its salespeople.

- To balance the results of every decision and action so that harmony is maintained between the short-range and the long-range goals of both the district and the entire corporation of which the sales manager is a part.

The Role of Planning

Management goals are accomplished by planning, which is the process of deciding in advance what will be done to accomplish the goals. Obviously, the overall objective of a sales organization is to meet the volume objectives established for that unit. But volume objectives are merely the measure of relative profitability. The real rationale for meeting a sales objective is to produce the profit necessary for the firm to grow. A budget is merely a tool in the hands of management to aid in the achievement of the goal of "profitable volume."

Thus, for the planning period, usually 12 months, the budget becomes one of the targets of the sales unit. It gives the manager authority to commit funds for the day-to-day operations of the district. Because these targeted funds become fixed for the period to be measured, the budget becomes three things: a control device, a management tool for action, and a measure of the effectiveness of management in attaining goals.

The Budget as a Cost Control.   One aspect of control is finding out whether business operations are being carried out according to management's plans. Control requires an orderly plan against which results can be measured. That is, you can see from the budget whether your operation is out of control and, if so, by how much and perhaps where.

A budget is based on a combination of historical cost trends, wishes for the future, and assumptions about a number of external happenings that will affect the validity of that plan. For example, a budget will have to take into account what the new union contract will mean in terms of increased base salaries of nonunion employees, including possibly the sales force, or whether travel or phone costs will continue to increase at the same rate as last year.

For this reason, a budget is not an inflexible policy statement, but a standard. When variances occur, they may indicate real trouble or they may merely be an exception. What caused the variance? Maybe the budget was based on faulty assumptions to begin with. This may make for 11 months of variance but does not destroy the validity of budgeting. A standard must remain fixed, or there will be no reference point.

The Budget as a Sales Control.   Everything that has been said regarding the place of financial controls in the measurement of manager effectiveness can also apply to the individual members of the sales force. It is part of territory management. Salespeople who are now required to maintain expenses within set limits and turn in weekly or monthly expense reports already have financial controls. In some instances, a manager may wish to extend such controls to include telephone expense, office supplies, or even a share of total office operating expenses. What is covered should, however, be readily measurable and under the control of the salesmen.

> Ed Smith is setting annual sales objectives for each salesperson reporting to him. He also establishes weekly expense limits, which vary from territory to territory depending on the geography and the types of accounts therein. Joyce Evans, one of the representatives in the district, has a travel and entertainment expense budget of $180 each week, which Ed averages over the month and the quarter to measure how well she is meeting financial goals.

We will look more closely at the use of such tools in the following chapter.

The Budget as a Management Tool for Action.   If the budget is balanced with respect to overall goals, then the budget becomes a part of the manager's plan either to keep the district in a status-quo condition or to push aggressively ahead. If a budget gets out of control, a 12-month tightening period or drastic surgery may be needed to get it back into shape. Unfortunately, experience has not shown us how to bring an out-of-control budget back on track in a short period. Time is often the only cure and is something seldom available. This is why budget control is so important: If expenditures go wrong, they must be caught and corrected without delay; next quarter may already be too late.

The Budget as a Measure of Management Effectiveness.
Budget control operates on the concept of "management by exception." This valid management principle helps conserve the manager's time and focuses it on those areas that should receive attention.

> The budget for the southeast district was on target, yet the line for travel expense showed an increasing "overbudget" trend for the past three months. The question is not one of being "within budget," but one of why travel expenses were suddenly "out of control." Note that the item was deemed to be out of control over a three-month time span, because one month does not set the pattern; rather, the trend sets the pattern.

This is management by exception. The reasons for the negative trend and what action the sales manager is taking are measures of management effectiveness. The travel expense trend indicates the area that needs the attention.

The Different Elements of the Budget

In any budget, some items are fixed, and some are variable. That is just the nature of costs. In a production budget, for example, the cost of leasing equipment is fixed, but the operating costs of that equipment can vary with output or use. In a sales budget, the lease cost of a company car is fixed, while the cost of gas and often repairs varies with use and condition.

On the other hand, as any sales manager is aware, fixed costs are only relatively fixed, and variable costs seldom do vary. Salaries are fixed, but if a sales territory is closed and the salesman laid off, the expense, except for the cost of separation, is eliminated. Travel expenses are variable, but to what degree? Where is the point of diminishing returns and diminishing sales?

So we must find a different terminology to effectively segregate the various budget elements into more meaningful categories:

- *Committed costs.* These are the costs over which the sales manager has little direct control once they are undertaken or committed. Such costs as rent, salaries, or any item under contract fall into this category. Also included are certain employee benefits, car leases, and basic telephone system costs up to a minimum usage level. Over the long run, such charges can vary with changes in corporate direction and policy, but they do not respond to the day-to-day operating decisions of the sales manager, nor do they fluctuate with changes in sales volume.

- *Managed costs.* These costs can be controlled to some degree by the sales manager. Such costs as telephone bills for long-distance calls or the number of calls over a minimum are in this category. Such costs as office supplies, sample usage, entertainment expense, and travel can be managed for the individual sales territories.

Measuring the Cost Function

The Jason Company breaks down monthly department profit and loss statements to reflect variances from budget for each line of expense for the sales force. In addition, expenses are grouped into categories of committed cost, managed cost, and product cost, which sales districts "purchase" from the manufacturing units at a standard that allows sales units to be measured on a "profit" basis.

When given a measure of his sales-cost-profit performance, the manager has the tool to control total performance. When a manager finds that variances are out of control, there are only a limited number of places to look for correction:

- When the margin between selling price and product cost, even simulated product cost, falls, it often indicates the need to increase the selling price.
- Every unit has a calculable breakeven point, which can be changed in one of three ways: by varying the selling price, by changing variable cost elements, or by changing fixed costs. Yet in most instances, it is not fixed cost that is controllable, but only the managed-cost portion of the fixed elements of cost.
- The relationship between what is spent and the results obtained may be out of control. If this element is indeed out of control, it can be changed only by drastic surgery. At times, the cut may need to be made not in the offending line of the budget, but someplace else. The objective is the balanced budget, not the detail line.

Whether or not a manager is in a position to take the necessary actions to increase unit profits in his unit, the budget is an important clue to the overall health and continued growth of that unit. A sales manager may know that in order to improve operations—increase profits—more should be spent on travel and entertainment. But according to the overall company plan, this may not be feasible. The sales manager still has the responsibility to understand what is happening and what may be needed, even if the final decision is not his.

The Budget in Perspective

Now, let's go back to those opening remarks by various managers and examine them in light of everything that has been said up to this point about the budgeting process.

"The measure of a manager is the ability to meet the budget." Most sales managers do not see how their operation relates to the total profit picture. The effect of sales and expenditures is outside the functioning of individual sales districts. Their major contribution to the total can therefore be measured only by expenditures against individual budgets, which unfortunately leaves the budget to be the measure of the manager. Individual sales budgets are most meaningful when they are validated by total corporate expenditures and related to total corporate sales.

"A budget is a road map." When put into its proper context, the budget becomes a part of a dynamic whole that makes up a measure of the total effectiveness of the individual sales manager. It is never the budget that is out of control, except as it helps management evaluate the whole.

"I'm more concerned with the bottom line, not the individual items of the budget." The bottom line measures the success of the sales unit. If the individual lines of the budget are on target, the bottom line is on target. What is important is that the manager has not weakened his contribution to the success of the entire firm in trying to meet the budget. For example, a sales manager may be able to stay within the guidelines of the budget by not allowing his salespeople to increase entertainment expenses, since other lines of the budget are "out of control." But what is that decision going to do to the total sales picture? Not that the decision is necessarily wrong, but is there a better decision?

"No manager can manage only one aspect of the job." Budgeting is a measure of management ability, but it is only one objective against which the manager should be measured.

Each of these managers is correct in his statement. A budget is merely a tool in the hands of a manager, and its effectiveness depends directly on the use that the manager makes of it. Today's managed expenditures are tomorrow's profit, but they may also be today's loss. There are no formulas for making decisions regarding managed expenditures. They must always be based on judgment and are almost always a compromise. Any fool can stay within a budget; it takes a manager to balance the divergent needs of a sales organization.

Looking Back; Looking Ahead

The foregoing, then, represents the crust of the pie that holds together and supports all that is management. We began this book by introducing the "gap" approach in the first chapter, even though it might more logically seem to be a part of planning and setting objectives. At the same time, it is a logical beginning, since you can neither plan nor set objectives until you know where you want to go. Without knowing where you want to go, you can never know when you have arrived. Without a map, one route will be as good as any other.

For the field sales manager, the elements of planning are relatively basic. You must give direction to the sales force, collectively and individually. Since all salespeople are faced with the objective of being managers of their assigned territories, planned coverage is essential. The question is reasonably easy: "How do you plan to cover this territory most effectively?"

Thus comes the need to establish objectives for each of the territories—objectives that, as we saw, are measurable. Objectives are both specific, in terms of their being short-range stepping-stones to a greater goal, and financial, as dictated by the elements of good budgeting. Such objectives give direction to territory management and control to the sales manager.

This, then, formed the crust of our pie.

Looking ahead, it is necessary that we begin to fill that crust. In the next chapter, we will continue with what has been presented herein by showing you, in effect, what to do with the plans and objectives. Plans merely get you into things; it takes the actions of supervision and control to make the plans work. In the following chapters, we will add the filling to the pie as we discuss the means the sales manager has available to implement the objectives that were established.

Finally, before we finish, we will put a rich topping on our pie as we look at some important reasons why salesmen fail and what can be done about it.

Right now, let's begin to add the filling.

4

Supervision and Control: How Do I Keep It Going?

How salespeople go about accomplishing their goals should, perhaps, not be analyzed too closely. What is finally accomplished is the real standard of performance.

There should be no argument with such a statement. It is true. Unfortunately, what is missing is the assurance that the sales force, the entire sales force, will return 100 percent effectiveness; will need no policy interpretation; will, in effect, not need any management at all. In other words, if we accept the above statement as not only true but true to life, then it implies a chief executive and thousands of workers and salespeople all doing their thing. Tell me why this is ridiculous and you will have defined management.

Now we understand why we exist as managers. Management, having established the objectives for the sales force, is required to do whatever is necessary to see that these objectives are accomplished, are completed on time, and are met with a minimum of cost or lost productivity. That is called, in two words, supervision and control.

Perhaps above all, the need to measure more than the final result is the essence of the supervising function. The sales manager needs to know how things stand along the route that begins with the setting of objectives and ends, some 12 months later, with the final annual result. To accomplish this measurement, managers need a number of tools, all of which exist to aid them because of a common human failing: No manager is good enough to supervise on instinct alone.

The Tools of
Supervision and Control

Essentially, anything that helps you to measure what is happening in the world that is your responsibility is a tool. What we want to examine specifically at this time are several of the more common tools at your command. What I am saying is that when we finish with this chapter, we will not have presented an all-inclusive list of management tools, only a few suggestions built around the more common and useful ones, which are presented for your use, with the hope that a variety of other similar tools will suggest themselves to you as you search for answers to the problems of control. Yet this is exactly where the tools introduced herein came from originally. Each was created to solve a management problem.

The Abhorrent Call Report

Once upon a time, Joseph Cawle, the sales manager for a major corporation, awoke to the realization that he did not know where any of his salespeople would be that day, or the day before, or the day before that. (This is a true story; only the facts have been changed.) Rushing to his office, he decreed that henceforth all salespeople would submit two weekly letters: one to list every place they would go next and the other to list every place they had been the week before. These lists came to be known as the Cawle (pronounced "call") report.

This was, as we said, a long time ago. But the Joseph Cawles of the selling world were so impressed with the simplicity of the report that it remained virtually unchanged up until the present moment. Oh, with the invention of the printing press, some efficiency-minded managers decided to standardize on various forms, but the basic concept remained intact.

Then, some years ago, a group of well-meaning but nosy staff assistants pointed out that for some time, ever since sales management had become infatuated with setting objectives, the call report (as it came to be known) could be used to count the number of calls made by each salesperson. Thus, it became much easier to measure activity than to measure results.

However, for a long time, this left the call report basking in nothing but glory, since management could point out that it was an effective control tool. If five calls each day were what was wanted, there were five calls per day on the call reports of all but the newest and least experienced salespeople—which was another method of measuring how they were improving in their selling effort. If management felt that companies of a certain potential demanded one call each week, call reports from all over the nation reflected religiously one call per week on such accounts. And so the call report ceased to be a viable instrument. As a matter of fact, until recently, only those firms that had apparently printed an oversupply of the forms were even requiring them, and no one read them anymore—which was all right with the sales force.

The Call-Planning Report

It does not have to be like this. In a minute, I am going to introduce one possible version of a call report—the call-planning and activity report—which I have used successfully for a number of years. You will find it reproduced in Figure 8 later in this chapter, and I will use it to illustrate how it can again become a viable means of control for the sales manager. Please note: It is not the form that is viable, but the use to which it is put. Thus, before we look at its use, let me present a philosophy of call planning. I will begin with the following position statements:

Planned direction is the most effective means of achieving a desired result. To use available time effectively, the salesman must establish priorities for that time. Said simply, salesmen need a list of where they are planning to go.

We once did a "time and duty" study of the daily selling activities of a group of industrial sales engineers. The results showed that, on the average, these salesmen spent less than 20 percent of their selling time in face-to-face contact with a prospective buyer. That is probably an extreme, considering the type of equipment being sold, but it points up the problem facing all salesmen—that of being frugal, even stingy, with the time they have available to them. Time is the only resource a salesman has!

Every sales call should have an objective. Unless a salesman has a specific reason for making a sales call, he cannot measure the success of that call. Even a cold call has an objective. Unfortunately, we tend to accept just "seeing if they are using my type of product" as a viable reason or objective. It is not complete as it stands. It is not enough. It does not justify the time required for the call. What else will we have to accomplish to make this an effective call?

> "Well, I really want to talk to someone in the engineering department so I can demonstrate my product, and I want to leave a catalog with both engineering and purchasing, but only if the volume of product they will use justifies it."

All right! There are your objectives on this cold call. If you do not accomplish all these things, you have not achieved your objective. Therefore, in planning where to call, you must also know the reason for the call or it has not been properly and effectively planned.

The foregoing two steps become the planning portion of a call. From the plan follows the action.

Regardless of what happens on a sales call, whether effective or ineffective, these two steps are what will form the basis for continuing sales strategy. At times, the salesman's list of plans will change. Buyers forget, meetings run longer than intended, weather gets in the way, competition reacts or counterreacts, more facts turn up. Many controllable and uncontrollable factors become a part of the result of any planned activity. Thus, if "what happened" is to be useful in developing future tactics or follow-up, three questions must be answered for each call:

1. What happened when you made that call?
2. What will you do next?
3. When will you do this?

When your people can respond accurately to such questions, you have the essential data around which a call-planning and activity-reporting procedure can be built. Reproduced in Figure 8 is a form that resulted from an attempt to give the sales force a means of summarizing the needed information. It is not offered as an example of either the best or the only way of constructing such a

Figure 8. A call-planning and activity report form.

SALES ITINERARY PLANNING/ACTIVITY REPORT

| Representative | Week |
| Territory | Region |

TRAVEL PLAN
(City/State)

Monday ___ Tuesday ___
Thursday ___ Friday ___
Wednesday ___

CONTACT PLANNED: (person/account)	CITY	OBJECTIVE	CC	TC	CALL COMMENTS	NEXT TACTIC	DATE

MONDAY

TUESDAY

CONTACT CODE: P – Phone contact N – Negotiation S – Service call I – Customer information request
U – Unclassified call

TOPIC CODE:
Designate product code

CONTACT PLANNED: (Person/account)	CITY	OBJECTIVE	CC	TC	CALL COMMENTS	NEXT TACTIC	DATE
WEDNESDAY							
THURSDAY							
FRIDAY							

form. In a sense, it is even rather clumsy, in that it requires the salesperson to either recopy or duplicate information (if used first as a plan and next as a report of results). However, it has worked well for me in three companies and is also used by a number of other managers who have asked for help in developing the data it presents. What I am saying is that to date I have not found a better method.

I want to show you some examples of how such a form can be used. Before doing so, however, let's talk about the call-planning form itself.

Sales Itinerary Planning/Activity Report. The left portion of the form represents the plan. By the end of the previous week, the salesman is required to plan the major call schedule for the week to follow. The essential information to be included would cover who he plans to contact, the location, and the reason for the contact. Additional information is coded to clarify possible objectives and to simplify filling out the form.

For example, the "contact code" indicates the type of call planned. An *N* (negotiation) designates a key or major sales effort, usually where the order is achieved following a series of calls and involves a specific sales volume (say, over $50,000). A service call (*S*) indicates a trouble call or a follow-up call where no major negotiation is underway. *I* (customer information request) indicates a call made in response to a customer request that has not yet been identified as a specific sales call or key negotiation. All other calls are grouped as unclassified, *U*. These include cold calls, although a manager may want to segregate these further or designate different codes to meet specific requirements or industry terminology.

Phone calls (*P*) do not normally belong on a planning report. For that matter, it might be argued that they really do not belong on the call report at all. However, as you will see, the report also serves as a communication update for the sales manager, and the phone classification indicates just that, perhaps adding vital information or an update on an activity's status to keep management advised of a pending situation. It thus becomes a special class of call.

Finally, in the upper right hand corner of the first page, the salesman outlines his travel itinerary for the coming week. This can be used in several ways. Since the "planned" portion of the report is completed and a copy mailed to the sales manager by the end of the previous week, it also keeps the sales manager informed of where the salesman might be contacted, other than by leaving a message with the office or answering service. Again, we are not establishing a form design but making suggestions that might show you the use of such an instrument. But it must be modified to meet your specific needs.

Figure 9 illustrates a portion of John Smith's planning report. Note that he has indicated where he will probably be staying during the week. As the week progresses, John will fill in the activity portion of the form. By the end of the week, the completed form, along with the plan for the subsequent week, will be mailed to his sales manager.

The Call Report in Action. Besides providing the sales manager with a tool for knowing where the sales force is going to be, the plan gives the manager an insight into the way each salesperson tends to view his individual territory. Certainly, a single report is not sufficient, but over a period of several weeks, the manager, by knowing something of both the sales personality involved and the territory in question, can spot a number of trends.

It can become apparent when the salesman is floundering. The same customers begin appearing over and over, with little indication of a strategic reason. Too many new names at random could indicate that the salesman is approaching his territory planning without telephone prospecting—merely making calls in the hope that something will turn up. Perhaps this is not serious in itself, but it indicates a potential danger area, and the knowing manager looks for such trends as a tip-off before they do become serious.

If each salesperson has indicated a territory coverage plan, the call report will tell you if it is being followed.

Another important trouble area can be spotted through the call pattern on key negotiations. Typically, a key negotiation is what will form the basis for the salesperson's meeting a "gap" situation. Do the scheduled calls over a series of weeks indicate adequate coverage of these targeted customers?

Finally, the call-planning report tells the sales manager that there is a plan. There is always the danger that we will begin to measure activity rather than results. That is not the intent of control. Perhaps another way of stating this would be to say that it is

Figure 9. John Smith: Call-planning report.

SALES ITINERARY PLANNING/ACTIVITY REPORT

Representative: John Smith
Week: 5/7 - 5/11
Territory: 5
Region: Mid-central

TRAVEL PLAN (City/State)

Monday	Tuesday	Wednesday	Thursday	Friday
Springfield / St. Louis	STL Airport Holiday Inn	STL	Jeff City - STL	Office

CONTACT PLANNED: (person/account)	CITY	OBJECTIVE	CC	TC	CALL COMMENTS	NEXT TACTIC	DATE
MONDAY							
Calabelly-Hamon Purch.	Peoria	Present quote	N	A			
Springfield Elec.	Springfield	drop-off samples	S	Y			
Central Control Dallas Chief Eng.	Springfield	demo H line	I	H			
TUESDAY							
Barth Amd.-Lunch	St. Louis	ad request	I	A			
Monsanto-Knupt	STL	pick up order, discuss del. sch.	N	H			
Emerson Elec.-Lunch	STL	will they go ahead?	N	A			
Michael Bros-Eng.	STL	determine need	U	H			

CONTACT CODE: P – Phone contact N – Negotiation S – Service call I – Customer information request
U – Unclassified call

TOPIC CODE:
Designate product code

not the number of calls, but the quality of calls—the booked orders. This is what measures results. Planning merely gets us to this point.

Figure 10 shows a portion of the completed call report submitted by John Smith at the end of the week. Note the comments indicating what turned out to have happened, the action taken, and the timing of the follow-up.

Not all accounts that will be called on will appear on the planned-call portion of the schedule. Only key customers are important, although all scheduled calls should be indicated if they are known. Notice that WABCO in Peoria was added, probably because time became available. In addition, the report shows that a phone contact on Tuesday followed up with details missed on that Monday call to WABCO.

Space on a form will not always permit a full explanation of events. Therefore, there will be times when the action taken, the tactic, or even the call objective will appear cryptic or unclear. Such items can readily be circled and set aside for further discussion when contact is next made with the salesperson.

Although my experience is not necessarily the rule, I find that I can use a salesman's call report at the end of each quarter to help me prepare for a review with him.

Take a legal-size tablet and crisscross it horizontally and vertically, dividing it into 12 blocks, representing the first 12 weeks of a quarter. (Yes, I realize there are 13 weeks, but it is easier to work with even blocks.) If you now list each customer and location by name, using each block to represent one week, you will have outlined the salesperson's call pattern for the quarter. Individual accounts can be connected with lines to form a call pattern. Total territory coverage can thus be readily scanned and discussed with the salesperson in an effort at possible improvement or developing a new strategy as the need arises.

How Many Calls a Day?

If you average the number of calls a day or a week, and we all do it, then do not tell the sales force you do. Nothing will kill a call-reporting system faster than for the sales force to think that the number of calls is important. It is in fact not the number of calls that is important, as I have attempted to stress before; it is the

Figure 10. John Smith: Call-activity report.

SALES ITINERARY PLANNING/ACTIVITY REPORT

Representative: *John Smith*

Week: *5/7 – 5/11*

Territory: *5*

Region: *Mid-central*

TRAVEL PLAN (City/State)

Monday	Tuesday
Springfield St. Louis	*STL Augret Holiday Inn*

Wednesday	Thursday	Friday
STL	*Monday Jeff City - STL*	*office*

CONTACT PLANNED: (person/account)	CITY	OBJECTIVE	CC	TC	CALL COMMENTS	NEXT TACTIC	DATE
MONDAY							
Caterpillar-Human Pural.	Peoria	Present quota	UK	A	Looks good!	Follow for application call and disp. date	5/18
Springfield Elec.	Springfield	drop off samples	S	Y	Dist. salesman to present samples	Confirm joint calls	w/o 6/1
Central Control Books Chr. Engr	Springfield	demo H line	I	H	There is need— Engr. to review—	Set visit with engr. next trip	w/o 6/1
Walco—Serv. Mgr.	Peoria	Discuss parts stock	U	H	Need to reorder by end month	Pursh. not call	
TUESDAY							
Barth Ind.–Purch.	St. Louis	At request	I	A	Small usage—left brosh.	Call off dist. to follow	—
Monsanto-Kugut	STL	Pick up order Discuss del. sch.	N	H	PA sick order delayed	Confirm with secty for new call date	5/9
Emerson Elec Purch.	STL	Will they go ahead?	N	A	Decision not made—	Follow offor their communic. meeting	w/o 6/1
Michael Bros-Engr.	STL	Determine need	U	H	No current use	Send literature	—
Walco	Peoria	Get parts order	P	H	Phone order received	Called order service—	—

CONTACT CODE: P – Phone contact N – Negotiation S – Service call I – Customer information request
U – Unclassified call

TOPIC CODE:
Designate product code

effectiveness of the calls. More to the point, if you say you want 4 or 16 calls each day, you will get 4 or 16 calls each day. Just make sure that is what you really want!

The call-planning and activity report is a valuable information tool for both the salesman and the manager. As important as it may be for the manager, it becomes more essential as a tool for the individual salesperson. What I am saying is that if this tool is to remain valid, the sales manager must make it so in the minds of the sales force. They must learn to use the report to self-police their own efforts. The manager must take every opportunity to see that it becomes more than a weekly exercise. You do this by referring to the report regularly and by taking every opportunity to let the sales force see you using it. The reason is axiomatic: "What the manager thinks is important the manager pays attention to." Let the sales force see you stop using something and watch how quickly it falls into disuse. Salesmen are among the sharpest people on earth when it comes to reading clues in any situation.

There is, as always, an exception to the above comments about counting calls.

> I had been hired as sales manager for a group of salespeople who had extremely lax supervision in the past. They literally thought nothing of getting on a plane, having lunch with an account, and flying home. After several weeks, I had to insist on a minimum number of calls and let them know that I did indeed count them.

Key-Account Strategy

It is not that I have any more love for filling out forms than the next person, but I do respect the simplicity they can bring to the process of collecting and interpreting information. Thus, allow me to present another form.

Anytime you wish to summarize what is happening with a specific negotiation, there are certain things it is essential to know:

1. Who is the customer? Where is he located? (This is particularly relevant if the salesman covers a large area with several cities.)
2. If you sell multiple product lines, which one is the customer interested in buying?

3. What is the value of the negotiation? (This can be in terms of annual volume, units, or total purchase price.)
4. When do you expect the order to be awarded?
5. At this moment, what is the probability of the salesman successfully obtaining the order?
6. Is a third party involved (for example, a contractor, consultant, final end user, distributor)?
7. In what stage is the negotiation? (Has the need been established? Are the specs written? Has the quotation request been made? Is the negotiation now down to final details? And so on.)
8. What is the current situation? (What is happening within whatever stage the sale is at?)
9. What action is planned to ensure success? What is the next tactic?

This has led to the development of the "key-negotiation summary" form, shown in Figure 11. Each salesperson, upon entering into a key sales effort (for example, any negotiation or sales project over a specified amount), is required to attach a key-negotiation summary report with his weekly call report. This notifies the sales manager of the pending sales effort and triggers a discussion of each negotiation from time to time to update the form. Comments made by the salesperson during a phone conversation or a visit by the sales manager to the territory or on the call-activity report can be added to the form under the comments section. The net result is that the sales manager has an active file at all times with updated information on the major sales activities in the district or region.

Determining the Negotiation Stage. A study of the selling/buying process shows that all purchasing effort goes through a series of separate and identifiable steps or stages. Although these differ from industry to industry, and even from customer to customer, ten steps or stages tend to cover most situations—enough so that we can identify them on a general form for a day-to-day discussion of the status of a particular sale. These ten stages, which are discussed in detail in the text *Advanced Industrial Selling* (AMACOM, 1981), have been incorporated into the key-negotiaion summary form presented in this chapter.

Figure 11. Key-negotiation summary form.

KEY – NEGOTIATION SUMMARY

REPRESENTATIVE	CUSTOMER	LOCATION	PRODUCT	VALUE

THIRD PARTY (if involved)	ESTIMATE CLOSE	% CHANCE

Directions: On the top row of the grid, enter the date of your first negotiation with the client in the vertical column corresponding to the negotiation stage (as shown in the following list of stages). In the second horizontal row, enter the date of your second negotiation in the vertical row corresponding to that stage, and so on. Then, in the "Comments" section below, write each date again with a brief description of the transaction that occurred on that date.

1 2 3 4 5 6 7 8 9 10

1. recognize need
2. study solutions
3. decide to proceed — budget project
4. study products/suppliers
5. write specs
6. quotation request
7. submit bids
8. evaluation
9. negotiate terms
10. award order

COMMENTS

The Key-Negotiation Summary in Action. A series of key-negotiation summary reports is presented in Figures 12 through 14 to illustrate some of the uses a sales manager can make of the information supplied by the tabulation chart showing the "flow" of each sales effort.

Acme Tides Company. The value of the key-negotiation summary form is its ability to give a quick pictoral view of the status of a given sale. That, incidentally, is the value of all effective management tools—they provide a quick overview of trends. When trends do not tally, you begin to look more closely at what is happening.

As with any trend, you need time to develop enough data for it to become meaningful. However, it should have become rather obvious to the sales manager that the Acme Tides negotiation, illustrated in the key-negotiation summary form shown in Figure 12, was beginning to get into trouble on or about March 1, as competition managed to get the specifications changed. Unfortunately, trend data are after the fact by their very nature. Thus, by the time you see a sale in trouble, it is almost too late. On the other hand, when the salesman filed the Acme Tides negotiation report (see entry for March 1), it should also have alerted the manager to examine if the sales strategies being used would do the job. You do not have to wait until it is too late to begin a counteraction. A form such as the key-negotiation summary is there to help you think about what is happening as it happens.

Looking at the March 5 and March 15 entries, it appears the selling skills of the salesman might be questioned. Otherwise, how do you go from an optimistic 80 percent success probability to a lost order in a little over one week?

While the trends themselves may not have given enough advance warning for the sales managers to react, such information, even regarding lost orders, becomes important in retrospect. A discussion with the salesman examining what went wrong can build future successes. Such a postmortem will also show the sales manager what should have been probed with the salesman earlier in the sale.

Baker Parts Company. Here, as illustrated in Figure 13, is a negotiation that progresses logically from the first. Looking back over the flow of the sale, it can be seen to tie in logically with the comments made and the strategy and tactics used. Even the im-

Figure 12. Key-negotiation summary: Acme Tides Company.

KEY – NEGOTIATION SUMMARY

William Robinson   *Acme Tides*   *Centerville*   *H line*   *$50,000*
REPRESENTATIVE   CUSTOMER   LOCATION   PRODUCT   VALUE

_____   *2Q*   *50 80 60*
THIRD PARTY (if involved)   ESTIMATE   % CHANCE
                               CLOSE

Directions: On the top row of the grid, enter the date of your first negotiation with
the client in the vertical column corresponding to the negotiation stage (as shown in
the following list of stages). In the second horizontal row, enter the date of your
second negotiation in the vertical row corresponding to that stage, and so on. Then,
in the "Comments" section below, write each date again with a brief description of
the transaction that occurred on that date.

1   2   3   4   5   6   7   8   9   10

			1/10						
						2/11			
			3/1 →	3/1					
						3/10			

1. recognize need
2. study solutions
3. decide to proceed – budget project
4. study products/suppliers
5. write specs
6. quotation request
7. submit bids
8. evaluation
9. negotiate terms
10. award order

COMMENTS

1/10 *Presented samples - Engineer will test*

2/11 *Specs open - our prices high - proposed alternative*

3/1 *Competition got specs changed - Both our size and*
     price a problem

3/5 *We cut price - Buyer pleased - 80% chance*

3/10 *Negotiation delayed - buyer traveling*

3/15 *Lost on price*

Figure 13. Key-negotiation summary: Baker Parts Company.

KEY – NEGOTIATION SUMMARY

Greg Evans	*Baker Parts*	*Northway*	*ZB line*	*$70,000*
REPRESENTATIVE	CUSTOMER	LOCATION	PRODUCT	VALUE

Bass & Co.-Consultant	*3Q*	$\frac{80}{60}$ $\frac{}{50}$
THIRD PARTY (if involved)	ESTIMATE CLOSE	% CHANCE

Directions: On the top row of the grid, enter the date of your first negotiation with the client in the vertical column corresponding to the negotiation stage (as shown in the following list of stages). In the second horizontal row, enter the date of your second negotiation in the vertical row corresponding to that stage, and so on. Then, in the "Comments" section below, write each date again with a brief description of the transaction that occurred on that date.

1. recognize need
2. study solutions
3. decide to proceed — budget project
4. study products/suppliers
5. write specs
6. quotation request
7. submit bids
8. evaluation
9. negotiate terms
10. award order

COMMENTS

1/2 New application - customer checking reference installations

2/1 Good references - should move ahead in 2 wks: 60% chance

2/15 Plant visit with customer - 80% chance

3/1 Competition bid alternative - Consultant not favorable to us
        is coming in to evaluate bids

3/10 Plant visit for consultant favorable. Revising specs
        in our favor

3/20 Moved favorable evaluation to negotiation stage
        - will have order next week

proved probability of success, progressing from the initial 50 percent to 80 percent as the salesman's confidence in his tactics increased, appears reasonable enough to be accepted as being on the right track.

Following the competitive countermove on March 1, along with the entry of a third party into the evaluation of the bids, the flow can be seen to move backward to an earlier stage, where the strategy to achieve parity in the evaluation process becomes successful. In addition, the salesman managed to move the sale quickly to the final stage of negotiation and was awarded the order.

This example was included to show the strategy possibilities in a sale. The seller has a number of strategic options. The sale will normally progress naturally from step to step. Letting it proceed normally is one option. However, if the salesman does not feel in the best competitive position at any stage, he can develop a tactic for moving back to an earlier stage, from which the sale can be brought forward again more favorably. If in a particularly strong position, the salesman can develop a tactic to jump the sale ahead and take advantage of his current strength by keeping the competition off balance.

To be able to effectively quarterback the sale, the sales manager needs some means of seeing the overall strategy—of picturing what is happening. The key-negotiation summary form provides this picture.

Central Switch Company. Here is an entirely different picture. When you see such a stagnant picture as that illustrated in Figure 14, you can be sure the salesperson is not controlling the sales action. Additionally, noting the explanations being presented in the comments section, it would appear evident that Charlene does not have a strategy for meeting the challenges presented by this sale. It is up to the sales manager to help her develop that strategy. Since most successful selling strategies are brought into play in the earlier steps of a sale, it is important for the manager to be in a knowledgeable position in order to suggest alternative strategies as soon as possible. Once again, having a picture of the current sales situation is what allows the manager to help initiate a counterstrategy before it is too late to recover control in the sale.

It should again be stressed that I do not intend to suggest that the key-negotiation summary form presented herein is the only or the best option. I am suggesting, however, that the sales manager

Figure 14. Key-negotiation summary: Central Switch Company.

KEY - NEGOTIATION SUMMARY

Charlene Wilson	*Central Switch*	*Southtown*	*A line*	*$85,000*
REPRESENTATIVE	CUSTOMER	LOCATION	PRODUCT	VALUE

	3Q	*25%*
THIRD PARTY (if involved)	ESTIMATE CLOSE	% CHANCE

Directions: On the top row of the grid, enter the date of your first negotiation with the client in the vertical column corresponding to the negotiation stage (as shown in the following list of stages). In the second horizontal row, enter the date of your second negotiation in the vertical row corresponding to that stage, and so on. Then, in the "Comments" section below, write each date again with a brief description of the transaction that occurred on that date.

1   2   3   4   5   6   7   8   9   10

1/10									
2/10									
		3/10							
			4/10						
			5/10						

1. recognize need
2. study solutions
3. decide to proceed — budget project
4. study products/suppliers
5. write specs
6. quotation request
7. submit bids
8. evaluation
9. negotiate terms
10. award order

COMMENTS

1/10 New prototype - will study different solutions before deciding on final design direction

2/10 Project stalled - no change in status

3/10 Budget tight - may postpone until next year

4/10 Project released - strong competition - We offered a redesigned A line if approved.

5/10 No change - customer looking at different approaches.

does need to develop his own method of keeping on top of what is going on in the region.

Tracking Territory Expense Trends

Among the tools available to the sales manager to use in the supervision and control of the sales force is a method of tracking the expenses of the individual salespeople.

In the preceding chapter, we discussed how weekly or monthly expense objectives could be established. To use the budgeted objectives as a control tool, the sales manager must be able to see both where each sales territory stands in relation to that objective and what trend is projected. The week-to-week, month-to-month result can be readily plotted against the set objectives. As a matter of fact, any number of simple methods can be set up with this end in view. One such method is illustrated in Figure 15.

John Smith has an expense budget of $180 per week, exclusive of office supplies, car repairs, postage, telephone, and possibly some other items. In effect, John's manager has decided to measure only direct travel and entertainment expenses. Thus even though other charges such as the above appear on John's expense report, these are substracted from the gross expense in determining weekly averages.

To facilitate the control job, John's manager also elected to keep track of weekly costs in a number of other categories, even though they would not be subtracted from the gross. This helps the manager see at a glance why one week might vary from another. For example, note under "hotel" that there is shown the number of nights and the total hotel expense. Again, control does not lie in the week's expenses, but in the trends.

We note that John is running well under budget for the quarter. There is no trend indication that anything is out of control or potentially a problem.

Thus, we have indicated three possible tools that the sales manager can use to gain control: the call-planning and activity report, the key-negotiation summary, and a method for tracking expense trends. As noted earlier, these are only representative of the many—some simple, some more elaborate—that are available. The key to each lies in its ability to enable the manager to spot

Figure 15. Plotting weekly expense trends.

Salesman: John Smith
Territory #202
Weekly Budget - $180

week #		Gross Exp.	Plane/Car Rental	Meals	Hotel	Other	Entertainment
JAN 1	City	8466				OFF.SUP. 18	20
2	City	9240				TELE: 43	
3	Peoria - 2	14154 (ave $76)		28	1-41	AMS.SER./28	33
4	City	15270				CAR REP. 75	41
FEB 1	STL - 4	25770		71	3-164		33
2	City	3367 (ave $216)					
3	V.C. - 3	49091	150/124	62	3-105		22
4	City	15108				POSTAGE 17 TELE. 50	18
MAR 1	Springfield - 2	13648		32	1-53	OFF.SUP. 25	12
2	City	9075 (ave $140)				TELE 78	
3	City	16933				TIRES 102	18
4	STL - 3	44596	105/130	62	2-78		37
5	City	8940				POSTAGE 20	
		QTR ave $144					

Note: Averages are made up of gross expenses minus "other" expenses.

potentially troublesome trends. The ultimate solution still requires a management decision, demanding judgment and experience. As with all management tools, they merely point the way.

The Art of Delegation

One of the least understood principles of management is the art of delegation, or how to keep from grabbing the tiller as your helmsman heads for the reefs. Just as no salesperson can be excused from mastering the art of territory management, no sales manager exists who does not delegate. The very nature of the sales effort ensures this. Thus, the question is not whether to delegate, or even when, but how.

Delegation is an essential part of all levels of management in a business environment. It is the means by which managers get their jobs done and a tool for the development of future management replacements. Delegation is the art of "pushing management down the line" to the level of the person who is in the best position to get the job done. Neither a single sales district nor an entire firm can grow on the leadership of just one manager.

Yet no matter how much you pass on to those below you in the organizational structure—your sales force—you cannot escape the fact that the final authority and the final responsibility rest with you, the sales manager. If one of your salespeople pulls the No. 1 boner of the year, you can fire him, but you cannot duck the fact that you were responsible for what happened. Delegation and control go hand in hand. In the balance of this chapter, I want to address the relationship between the two.

Delegation and Objectives

The objectives of the total corporation are the sum total of the goals that the management team has set for itself and for its individual department organizations. The delegation of authority at each level of management gives the subordinate managers the power to help accomplish those objectives.

It is the spirit of teamwork within the total management team that determines whether these objectives will be met. It is the spirit of the management team that motivates, that calls up the reserves

of energy and determination needed to help the team do its best—
and there can be no management team without delegation.

Since sales managers cannot run their districts entirely on their
own, they must delegate some of their authority in order to concentrate on the things they do best—those tasks that belong to them
alone. The role of the sales manager is not to sell, but to accomplish—to lead, to teach, to direct.

A sales unit that does not progress, does not grow in productivity, soon becomes stagnant. There are usually certain similarities
that distinguish such departments from the more productive ones.
These signs also aid the manager in spotting a potential source of
trouble in his own department. In a stagnant unit,

- There is no actual planning, although there may be formal
  plans. But these plans are usually found carefully filed away
  with the rest of the corporate trivia called staff memos.
- There is rigid adherence to formal organizational guidelines.
  The sales manager from one division of a firm cannot communicate readily with the sales manager in another division
  on an informal basis to solve a common problem.
- Detailed attention is paid to status symbols such as name-
  plates, parking spaces, and the pecking order.

It becomes obvious in watching such departments that there is
also little delegation of authority by the manager in charge. If such
sales managers would allow their salespeople to "let loose," the
department might begin to grow. New ideas might be offered, and
the sales force—with an increased sense of purpose and responsibility—just might be found working harder at their own achievements. Delegation is the way to give salespeople self-determination
and the way to get the most out of them. Often, it's the only way.

Unfortunately, for delegation to work, the sales manager has
got to work at it, and not just pay lip service to the concepts.

Delegating Authority

When managers delegate, they vest their salespeople with a
portion of their own authority. They surrender some authority, but
not their responsibility. If they do not surrender authority, they do
not delegate. Yet, they always keep the power to take back the authority they have given over.

Whenever there is delegation of authority, three aspects of that delegation can be observed:

- The assignment of duties by a superior to a subordinate.
- The granting of permission (authority) to make commitments, use resources, and take all actions necessary to perform the duties assigned (obviously, with any limitations also specified).
- The creation of an obligation or responsibility on the part of each subordinate to perform the delegated duties satisfactorily—and ultimately to stand answerable to the manager who has delegated that authority.

Learning to delegate authority effectively is an art. How it is done depends on the superior's management style. But whatever that style, the manager must be willing to give the salesman a chance. The superior must also be willing to let him fall flat on his face.

There are managers who prefer to make all managerial decisions personally. In so doing, they are unable to spend their time on the broader duties of their position. This often occurs with managers who have been promoted from one position to a higher position within the same functional unit. Good salesmen become sales managers, and if, in the process, they also become "supersalesmen" they may continue to hold tight to the authority of their position instead of being willing to delegate some of that authority to those who now work for them. As a result, the creativity of their sales people becomes stifled. Perhaps these managers fear letting go of the trappings of the position. Perhaps they just find it easier to be busy with what they know best.

Responsibility

There is a further problem with delegation—the problem of retained responsibility. One of the failings of management thinking in the past has been to put too much stress on delegating authority without being fully aware of the necessity for accepting responsibility for what has been given away.

It is important for managers to delegate authority, but it is equally important for them to assume responsibility for results. This is the first step in keeping the delegation of the authority in check. For instance, although higher management in a company (the sales director) may delegate authority to a sales manager to enable him to perform the functions of a sales manager, and the manager, in turn, may himself delegate, neither of them gives away any portion of his responsibility for the final result. When the director is called upon by his superior to explain a failure in the sales manager's district, the director cannot plead as a defense that he has delegated the responsibility. This is the difficult part of delegation. Authority can be delegated, but responsibility cannot.

There also appears to be a mistaken belief that even though managers are responsible for everything that goes on within their unit of authority, they may not act at a given moment if they have delegated away their specific authority. Again, this is a misunderstanding of the relationship between authority and responsibility. The decision to act always remains within a manager's sphere of influence, and the decision to give or take back authority is always his. But the moment the manager does take the authority back, this jeopardizes any future act of delegation on his part to the subordinate involved. Yet despite this double bind, managers must always be ready to take full responsibility for the actions of those reporting to them.

Another mistaken belief about the relationship between authority and responsibility is that authority and responsibility should be equal. This myth means that the sales force must have been delegated enough authority to undertake all the duties that they have been assigned and for which they have accepted responsibility to the delegating manager—but no more! This could lead to a stagnant, mechanized sales force. Even accepting this, how do you handle the salesman who continues to add to his responsibility, to assume increasing authority, and who, in case of doubt, never hesitates to take on decisions that are not being made by others perhaps more directly responsible? Such a salesman then has the responsibility, but without the authority. But that *is* the kind of subordinate you really want working for you, isn't it?

This sense of added responsibility can be found in capable workers at all levels. When it does show itself, it should be nurtured carefully. When sales managers let salesmen add to their responsibilities, the salesmen should also be ready to accept responsibility for their actions. This is implied delegation. I would much rather spend my time holding back salesmen than have to constantly be concerned with building a fire under them.

The Need for Control

It should be obvious by now that the manager who takes a chance and delegates authority to his salespeople is in a delicate position. The manager can never let the actions of the salesmen get out of hand or forget the objectives that must be accomplished. Thus the key to management control is to let the salesmen make decisions, but not without your knowledge. The coach of a football team does not run out onto the field when things get tough—and neither should you. Your job is to teach, observe, provide feedback—and only in a real emergency step in to make the decision yourself.

Controlling is a word with less than desirable overtones (like *reciprocal agreements, conglomerate,* or even *acquisition* or *merger*). Yet there is no reason this should be so. Controlling is as much a management function as planning, staffing, and supervising. Without control, we do not just have anarchy—we have lost the battle. Without control, there is no management. John Kenneth Galbraith, in *Economics, Peace, and Laughter,* discussed Eisenhower's success as a leader: "His rule was to keep one eye on the Germans, one eye on his generals, and both ears bent back toward Washington." The managerial equivalent of such a stance would appear to be highly recommendable for any manager, and it is the essence of control.

Methods of Control

As is true of all management techniques and principles, control will never be black-and-white, though it often takes specific form. It can be positive—directly applied and of necessity rigid. It can be relatively remote, self-policing, and more or less influenced by habit or peer-directed codes. It can be intentionally or unintentionally nonexistent. These are not prototypes of management behavior, but principles of action that any manager can make use of at any moment and in any specific situation to control that situation.

Simply put, control is the determination of whether business operations are being carried out according to management plans. Thus, bugeting, as we saw, is a control device. The "gap" approach, call reports, and any other tools that focus attention on the goals of the business become valid control devices.

Setting short-term objectives is an effective control tool, but so is setting even shorter-range objectives that can be accomplished in hours or days or weeks. In such circumstances, the manager constantly probes for answers or results. Failing to get them, the manager starts boring in, finding out everything he can about a particular problem area from anyone who might be involved. For this flow of information, the manager devises a reporting system or schedule and hammers it home until the set goal has been reached. If necessary, he can set another goal and, in stages of short, hard-hitting subgoals, reach for an even more elusive result.

> Gloria, a new sales representative for a speciality-equipment manufacturer, was assigned a sales territory covering Kentucky, Tennessee, and Alabama. This was an entirely new territory, not previously covered by any company personnel. In the past, business had primarily come from OEM sales, and now that industrial distribution had been decided on, it was felt the territory would support a sales rep.
>
> After several months, Gloria was frustraed at her own inability to locate enough OEM business to fill the "gap," even though that was not a primary need in this territory. Also, the distributors she had been able to sign up did not appear to be aggressively selling her line.
>
> Her manager understood Gloria's frustration, and the thoroughness of her digging for OEM potential had simply shown, as had in fact been expected, that the territory could not support sales on an OEM basis alone. To direct her energies toward developing the distribution side of her territory, the sales manager asked Gloria to contact all distributors and schedule at least two days of joint calls with the distributor salespeople. When this objective had been met, he had her call all large users directly to develop business that could be pulled through the distribution network. Meeting these short-term objectives developed a strong distributor group, whose sales began to take the place of the missing OEM volume.

During all of this, the sales manager was delegating action, demanding results, and controlling Gloria's overall sales effort.

The Importance of People

The real vigor in the life of a sales organization is what goes on among the salespeople who compose it. It has been accepted for some time that the worker in the shop, in all but the most automated operations, controls the ultimate pace and sphere of his job. Particularly in the office, any work of a clerical, skilled, or technical nature is governed by the will and the motivation of the individual. In the sales area, this control by the incumbent is practially absolute.

Controlling the sales force and their work under such conditions not only requires the principles of good management; it requires being "good at handling people." To be "good at handling people" does not imply a necessity to keep people happy. Even if it did, no sales manager would be able to achieve this feat. One person's happiness is another's misery. "Happiness is striped-colored walls!"

Actually the phrase "to be good at handling people" could better be worded, "to be good at interacting with people toward a common goal." The nature of each interaction would depend on the particular work situation and, more than that, on each particular salesperson involved. The interaction—and the management technique utilized—would obviously be different with a salesman who habitually failed to call his answering service than with one who consistently showed a sense of responsibility toward the job and territory.

In the former case, the use of fear or uncertainty about continued employment is a justified management tool. Using it as a blanket approach, however, not only is unjustified but can backfire. The manager who keeps the sales force "off balance" is guaranteeing a work group with growing resentment—a work group that will go out of its way to sabotage the manager, a work group in which emotional tension runs so high that productivity suffers.

The Types of Control

Every sales manager has at his disposal both positive and negative motivational techniques to use in controlling the sales force. The positive ones—encouraging teamwork, building an environment of trust and openness, and keeping emotional tension down—will give the best results. These are all techniques that we will investigate further in subsequent chapters. The negative techniques are best reserved for use when a salesman refuses to cooperate or deliberately breaks rules and challenges the manager's authority.

Mike resented his new sales manager. He felt the job should have gone to him. The sales manager was also concerned by Mike's attitude, particularly as it affected his sales performance. In several instances, the manager had talked to Mike about his work habit of not checking with the office for calls until late in the day. "I am going to insist on your checking in twice daily," Mike was told. "Get off my back!" he snapped. In a case like this, the sales manager has no choice except to stop such behavior in as firm a manner as necessary, including termination.

Depending on the situation, it is within the manager's options to work with a failing employee. You can explain, insist, and shout, but employees must take responsibility for the results of their own actions. Under no circumstances can the employees be allowed to harm the organization.

In building a spirit of teamwork, how far can a sales manager go in "becoming one of the troops"? Well, you cannot ever really be one of the troops because of the manager's power over the rest of the group—the power to recommend raises and promotion for them, the power to fire them. In fact, the manager who tries to become one of the troops usually makes the group uneasy precisely because of this power. The salespeople feel constrained not to say anything off the record around the manager because they feel, often justifiably so, that something they say may be held against them at a later time. Any open-door policy is really a myth.

But even though the fact of their position sets up a certain distance between managers and their sales force, managers can certainly be friendly, fair, and honest enough to level with them. They do not have to wear their authority like a cloak in their day-to-day dealings with the sales staff. The staff will always know it is there. Managers who constantly flaunt it are usually trying to reassure themselves, and their uncertainty actually undermines their positional authority.

> For years, I have made it a point to dine with my sales force on the occasion of a group meeting. Just as rigidly, I have also made it a rule to bow out early in the evening and let them go their way. You find you cannot successfully mix authority and fun in the long run.

The sales manager's relationship with the sales staff affects both the continued health and productivity of the department and the well-being of everyone who works for him or depends on the functioning of his sales unit. Every manager owes it to the sales force to use the control that is a part of his position for the sales staff's growth and future development. How the manager does this, however, is shaped by his own unique principles, feelings, and personality.

The Delicate Balance of Control

There is, of necessity, a delicate balance between delegation of authority and control, and it is not always easy to find the best way to achieve this balance.

Concerned managers will try to motivate their sales staff to take more and more responsibility, grow within their jobs, push for new ideas. They will enjoy the challenge that this gives them and hold themselves back from squelching the staff's enthusiasm, for they know that this is the only way of helping them grow.

Yet managers also know that if they let things get out of hand, progress will turn to chaos. After all, they are still the ones who will be called to task by their superiors if anything in their sales district goes wrong. But that is the nature of delegation. That is also what makes management an art rather than a science.

5

The Appraisal System: Is This Really Necessary?

The employee annual appraisal system does not appear to work very well in the great majority of companies. Yet we continue to pay homage to it because it is an important aspect of a human resources philosophy. If you doubt its significance, try to get one of your salespeople a salary increase without it. As a matter of fact, ignore it at the risk of your own managerial longevity.

It is not that managers do not understand what appraisal is all about. Most personnel departments are well equipped to provide manuals, slides, lectures, and promotional material to explain how it works and even why. Perhaps the difficulty is that it is so simple, no one really sits down and thinks it through as a total process— as a management tool. Instead, it becomes a procedure, something to "get through." So it ends up being an accumulation of forms and results in just "another annual review session." For the sales manager, the principles of management by objectives play an important role. Since most corporate appraisal systems also fill the basic requirements of MBO, it is necessary that the elements of both be understood.

MBO: The Great Management Myth

Marbreth Corporation has an established annual appraisal procedure based on the latest human resources procedures and theory. Each manager is required to discuss past performance with each employee in terms of specific areas of evaluation and the employee's job description and establish new objectives for the employees to accomplish prior to the next review. These objectives and areas of discussion are openly agreed upon with the employee, signed off by additional levels of corporate management, and filed in personnel department records to substantiate salary increase recommendations.

John Davis is a salesman in the firm's southern territory. His manager feels that John could increase his contribution to the region by becoming more involved with the engineering department personnel in his customer firms. (John agreed that he had a tendency to spend most of his selling time with purchasing people, thereby missing the opportunity to have his product specified in the firms' bids.) During John's annual performance review his manager used this as a point in evaluating John's performance.

This is not an example of management by objectives. Marbreth Corporation does not have an MBO program per se. Marbreth Corporation has an appraisal procedure.

In Chapter 3 we saw how we could establish standards of effectiveness that must be met in achieving job objectives. Carrying those standards to their point of measurement will result in an MBO program. Management by objectives is no more than structuring a procedure to set standards for, and record the outputs of, a salesman's job—in effect, measuring his performance against set objectives. It becomes an extension of the control process.

Here is a maxim that must apply to all effective control systems: "What cannot be compared to some standard—what cannot be weighed or counted or measured by some means—cannot be controlled." Thus, if you can establish standards for each of your salespeople that must be met in their overall efforts to attain their territory targets, then you have the basic elements for the development of an MBO program. As a matter of fact, you do have an MBO program, since the essence of MBO lies in establishing a series of short-term objectives building toward the larger objective of the sales territory—meeting quota.

The key to setting such short-term objectives lies foremost in their being specific—in their being measurable. It lies in their being comparable to some standard. Furthermore, such objectives contribute to the accomplishment of larger or longer-range goals. Let's look at some objectives.

Barbara sells medical equipment to hospitals and clinics. Her product line covers four basic categories:

1. Standard X-ray-room equipment, consisting of a basic tilting table, spot-film device, overhead tube stand, and generator.
2. A specialized line of tomography equipment.
3. A line of ultrasonic scanners.
4. A line of mammography scanners for breast examinations.

Barbara, in conjunction with her sales manager, had the following objective established at her last review: "to sell the complete line."

Georgia, working for the same firm in a different district, had this objective established during her review: "to meet the objective of selling the full line by closing at least one sale for each of the major product lines represented."

Helen, working for a third manager, had the following objectives established during her review: (1)"to obtain 80 percent of all current sales negotiations closing within the next four months"; (2) "to identify three new sales negotiations for ultrasonic equipment by the end of the quarter and present an acceptable strategy for competing in each negotiation."

Barbara is not involved with a workable MBO program. What constitutes a full line? For an effective MBO program, Barbara needs one or more short-term objectives. MBO is a growth-oriented plan. Growth comes only in increasingly improving increments.

Nor does Georgia have a workable MBO program. Georgia has a more specific objective than Barbara, and it could be used to develop an MBO program, but if Georgia's objectives are given typical treatment, they will not receive much more thought until the next review. That is not the intent of management by objectives (or management by anything!).

Helen *is* participating in an MBO program, whether consciously designed to be one or not. What makes the difference? Her objectives are short-term, specific, designed around her individual needs, and contribute to the overall job activity of "selling the complete line." Her objectives will change at the end of each short-term period and as she meets her present targets.

What we are looking for through an MBO program is job effectiveness, not merely efficiency. An efficient salesperson manages to accomplish a lot of things, but how well do those contribute to the territory results? Job position descriptions lead to efficiency, not effectiveness, because they deal with the "doing of things." It is, of course, assumed that when these things are done effectively, they will contribute to results. However, the job description, to my knowledge, does not specify measures or standards of performance. In other words, job descriptions are input-oriented rather than output-oriented—that is, results-oriented.

Traditional Approaches

In the opinion of the many sales managers I have worked with, performance appraisal has traditionally contributed little toward improving performance. Is it any wonder, then, that most performance appraisals are met with the same gleeful anticipation as would sitting in the center coach seat of a full airplane on a stormy, foggy Friday evening? It is something to be endured.

No one questions that if you are going to relate salary increases to performance, you should have some basis for justifying an increase. Likewise, there is little argument that such justification should be handled with some degree of consistency throughout a corporation. Thus it was, historically, that the idea of a common appraisal system developed primarily around the annual salary review. Unfortunately, early salary review programs did little to attract the endorsement of sales managers, much less managers from other functions. They were often, at best, rather uninspired compilations of what were undoubtedly thought of as factors of success. Many read like the Boy Scout oath—stating that a good salesman should figuratively, if not actually, be kind, brave, cheerful, and reverent.

> I recall my own efforts, not that many years ago, as a manager of marketing personnel development at Westinghouse, to construct an appraisal form that was not keyed to a series of personality factors. Industry has indeed come a long way.

Today, the forms used have gotten away from those measures that are not specifically job-related. Yet the forms and procedures—

and perhaps more important, the net results—remain almost exclusively part of an annual salary review program. This is all right, but when you view the system in such a light, you tend to miss its major contribution to the management of your staff: people development. The intent is there, but salespeople grow primarily through job results.

What I want to show you in this chapter is how to use a performance appraisal system for improving the productivity of your sales force without diminishing the effectiveness of its use for salary administration. Since you will probably have to use the present system in your firm for salary review anyway, why not build on it for your own purpose?

To accomplish this, we have to understand what makes a good appraisal interview. Thus, we will begin by entering into an appraisal review and watching the flow of the process. We will discuss some do's and don'ts and look at some of the techniques for getting where we want to go. Along the way, you can also examine some techniques that will make the appraisal process itself more effective.

The Appraisal Interview: From the Salesperson's Side!

Dear John:

My records show your anniversary date is due, and it will be necessary for us to schedule a performance review to complete the necessary paperwork. Since I will be making calls with you in your territory on June 18, let's plan to cover this review at the same time—perhaps following dinner that evening.

Ed Smith, Sales Manager

From the salesperson's point of view, the process begins at this point—regardless of the exact words or tone of the letter; regardless of whether the interview time is announced with a note or a phone call. *This is it!*

John let his mind drift back to the letter from time to time throughout the day. "I know I shouldn't let it get to me," he thought. "I remember last year. There wasn't really much to it, and Ed gave me a good rating. But I was 120 percent of quota that time. Now, with some of my key customers cutting inventories, I'm not going to look quite so good."

Psychologically, we are all troubled by one of two concerns: (1) We know we are good, but we are not sure others know how good we are; (2) we know we are not as good as would appear from the record, and we worry that others can see us for what we really are. Right or wrong, it builds tension.

What can we, as managers, do to eliminate this tension? Nothing, all the personnel manuals notwithstanding. If we do our managerial job, we are going to be critical. I do not care how objective both parties are. This is true in spite of the most blasé "doesn't bother me a bit, just let it all hang out" attitude. It is the nature of most people not to handle criticism well, even when the criticism is well intentioned and accurate. It builds tension. We can do some things to alleviate it, but that comes during the interview, not beforehand.

Preparing for the Interview Session

I do not want to talk too specifically about forms—primarily because there will not be much you can do about them. If your firm has a program, you will not be changing the form. If your company does not have a program, the form is not important. What we can talk about are those features of a good appraisal program that should be a part of your MBO endeavor, regardless of—or rather, in addition to—what is on the form. Philosophy is more important than the form used.

So we will start with three assumptions about what we might want from a performance appraisal system, particularly when used in conjunction with management by objectives:

- Since we are interested in rewarding performance, the net result should be improved productivity. We assume there is an interest in rewarding performance with such a system; otherwise, why bother with anything at all?
- Since rewards are for completed actions, we must look objectively at history: What has been done in the past to increase productivity?
- Since we do not reward productivity just to walk away from it when it has been achieved, the system must be the basis for focusing on future improvement beyond the originally specified point.

In essence, these assumptions are telling us that any workable performance appraisal system will cover the following areas:

What has the salesman done in terms of meeting past objectives—that is, performing in line with the functions of the job?

What will be expected in terms of future performance?

Anything additional you might find on an appraisal form either is there to expand on the above areas or is extraneous.

In preparing for the forthcoming interview mentioned earlier, Ed needs some factual information about John's performance since the last review. Among the performance data that are certainly of interest would be where John stands in relation to his sales targets and various product line quotas or even a record of his performance on specific customer accounts or in certain targeted industries. A second area would be John's specific performance against those short-term objectives that we discussed in a previous chapter and that are such a vital part of management by objectives.

Finally, Ed needs a list of the activities that are applicable to the sales position John fills. This is the sales job description, and while I am not being facetious, it is interesting to note the large numbers of salesmen, and even managers, who have never seen one. Why does such a condition exist in industry today? I would suspect it is because there is not much reason for the job description's being referred to. Everyone knows that a salesman's job simply comprises whatever activities it takes to get an order (legality and company policy considerations being assumed).

These data represent the past. In addition, there are two other areas that form the basis for the appraisal interview: the future and the salesman's personal expectations. What the appraisal process constitutes is in essence an examination of how John goes about achieving his objectives—how he has done so in the past and what is needed for the future. To be able to measure "how," Ed has to know what to look for. The "what" is inherent in the job description as well as in the question "What is a good salesman?"

What Is a Good Salesperson?

One of the activities performed by John is "to prospect—to search for new accounts." In thinking about this activity, a number of questions occur to Ed. His immediate reaction is that John is rather weak in this area. The call reports support such a feeling, showing a minimum of time spent in cold calling or telephone prospecting. In addition, those new accounts appearing on John's sales record have been developed from customers who have called to inquire about service, not, as far as Ed knows, from John's prospecting effort.

Ed feels justified in rating John "below-average" in this function. However, no salesperson operates within a single function. Ed will have to direct part of the appraisal session to the question of prospecting, but considering the entire picture of "John the salesman" brings additional questions into the picture.

John is considered one of the better salesmen in the district. He is consistently in the top quota. Having been in his territory for a number of years, he has developed a group of major customers who not only contribute to his sales volume on a regular basis but take up the bulk of John's time. As a matter of fact, Ed feels that when the subject is brought up in the review, John's response will be to question both the need for prospecting and how he would get the time to do more than he does.

Now we face a problem. Such questions are only easy to answer out of context. Yet as we have already noted, it is the entire salesperson who is being counseled and judged. Perhaps it is axiomatic that John must grow in the job—one of the three assumptions we made earlier. As with all assumptions, we have to look at the facts of the situation. We have to consider what John wants. However, my point is that the dilemma we have created can only be resolved by falling back on concept, on black-and-white—which is seldom the real world, but often the only way to solve the conflict.

Let me repeat. If you are going to keep the session from bogging down in the complexities of real life, then each function must be treated as independent of the others. Each must stand alone in its treatment. Ed must find the words to impress upon John the need for him to change his work habits. Then he must establish a new short-term objective, in agreement with John, that is aimed at improving this work area—or drop any further commentary on this function. If Ed does drop the subject, it is only because John "wants" and accepts such a lack of growth, since we already stated that Ed feels the function is important.

I am going to come back to this subject. For now, this is the only answer I can give. While there will always be circumstances in any situation that might justify tempering the answer, management must first respond to the concept. If you are going to make an exception to the concept in any decision, then do so knowing full well what you are doing. Management cannot manage by emotion—at least, not for very long.

This, then, is the preparation process. It demands that the manager examine each job activity of the salesperson, each previously established objective, and rate each in terms of the standards of acceptable performance for the position. What I hope has been clear is that the final value of the appraisal interview will be directly related to the planning effort given to it. When you have launched your canoe into the rapids, the time for planning is over. If you then say, "I don't know," the river will decide for you.

Beginning the Interview

If a rule of behavior does exist for the opening minutes of an appraisal interview, it has to lie in the fact that "everybody hates these interviews"—which is hardly a positive opening. It is up to the manager to set the stage by reducing the emotional tension of this first moment in a way that will lessen the salesman's inherent defensiveness and make him receptive to the communication that is to follow.

Unfortunately, most instructions at this point simply tell you to "help the other person to relax, possibly with some small talk." The fact is, the other person knows that is what you are doing, and the moment only becomes one of waiting for the shoe to drop.

Experience shows that the best opening is a businesslike approach to the session. That does not mean you cannot be pleasant. That does not mean you cannot provide for the salesman's comfort—offer coffee, close the door to ensure privacy. Through your words and actions, state the reasons for the review, putting it in a positive framework; set the agenda to be followed; and start!

Ed met John at the door to his hotel room with a warm smile. "Come on in, John. Take that chair by the table; I think it's more comfortable than the others." Ed has closed the door and shut off the TV set to add to the businesslike aura of the occasion.

"John, I haven't set any time limits on this. I think it is important for both of us to be able to just talk openly about a lot of things we don't seem to find the time to discuss on a more regular basis. So feel free to say anything you want to.

"I'm sure you're familiar with the review form we use" (assuming there is one), or, "Here's a list of the areas I want to cover."

Ed continues: "Here's how I suggest we go at this. As you are aware, an important reason for these discussions is to allow me to make a salary recommendation for you. That's important. But I also have another reason for getting together like this. This is my opportunity to bring myself up-to-date on all the things going on in your territory. I'm also interested in how you see your problem areas and what help you might feel you could use in resolving them. And of course, I want to try to answer any questions that you might have about what could be of concern to you."

Essentially, with words such as these or of a similar nature, Ed will try to set the ground rules for the discussion, to give it a direction. But he will also attempt to allay whatever fears exist and present as relaxing an environment as possible.

"So why don't we begin with those objectives we agreed to last quarter. I'll just review them, and then we will take them one at a time. Let's see, we had two targets: You were going to concentrate on developing H-line sales by 50 percent each quarter until you were on quota, and you were going to identify three new major sales negotiations through your prospecting activities. How are you coming with these?"

Here I have to make two important points. First, Ed certainly should know where John stands in accomplishing both these objectives. However, by letting John begin by talking about his own accomplishments or failures, Ed is giving John a chance to figuratively assume control (figuratively, not really, since Ed has chosen the topic and will have the chance for rebuttal when he replies to whatever stand John takes). Getting John to talk early in the review session is important. It shows John that this is not going to be a one-sided lecture, and it allows John to express the rationale for his own position.

Second, it points up the importance of having previously established those short-term objectives that we discussed earlier. Those short-term objectives are specific. Without them to open the discussion, you would be left having to begin with how well John feels he has performed the activities inherent in his position as a salesman. Without them, Ed's opening question might sound like this:

> "John, let's begin with a look at some sales activities. Prospecting is one. How has your development of new accounts been?"
>
> John flips his hand as if brushing the question aside. "Ed, you know the situation in my territory. I've got just about every minute taken up with major customers, such as BRW and Acme. My prospecting has to take a lower priority. But where I have the time, I'm as good as anyone. Don't forget, I had to develop those original accounts. I don't see how you can pin any realistic rating on that area, not for me."

Just in case you think I might have rigged that one, let's take a look at another version of the interview's opening moments—in the absence of short-range objectives:

> "John, let's begin with a look at how well you are calling on all of the different buying influences—engineering and key management people as well as purchasing."
>
> "Well, Ed, you know from making calls with me that I get around in all my accounts. I make it a point to develop these influences."
>
> "John, I'm going to take exception to that. When we were almost written out of the spec at Republic, you hadn't been close enough to what the engineering group was thinking to catch the problem until it was almost too late."

What is happening? No matter how you phrase your opening, you are faced with dealing with abstractions. That is the nature of job functions. You pointed out one area where John missed on a function, but John is not ready to accept that area as being representative of that activity. Only specific objectives are goal-oriented.

Thus, you end up dealing with emotions. Your opinion against his. Not a very good start for an open discussion.

However, assuming you did begin the review with a discussion of several specific objectives, these would probably cover only some of the salesman's job functions. How do you handle the other activities? Are you not faced with dealing on the same emotional level as before? The answer is yes. But consider that until the moment of this review, all other job functions carried a lesser priority than those functions around which objectives had previously been set. If John had a specific objective aimed at his prospecting function, then the review deals with how effectively John performed against the standard that was established at that time.

When the objectives and their related functions have been discussed, it is time to move the discussion into the areas of the other functions. Since you have now expanded the discussion into an area where no objectives previously existed, the discussion does start with emotion. In the end, it must come back to specifics—to results.

This is what it always comes back to. The goal is always productivity. Always effectiveness. We tend to measure activities when we should measure results. Prospecting is not important in itself. No individual function is. How much more effective John can be if he increases his prospecting *is* an important question. Then what should follow is the specific behavior change that will make him more effective. Since the final result must relate to the potential productivity of the sales job, you must have the job description as a basis. The ratings merely show you what areas need emphasis.

From Job Activities to Behavior

"John, here's how I rated your performance in each of the areas that should be important to your job as a salesman." Or, "Here's how I rated each activity on your job description. Let's discuss each in turn. I'll give you my reasons, and I'd like to hear your reasons and the way you would rate yourself."

"Ed, I'll have to agree with all your ratings except for the area of prospecting. I would have rated that at least a 6 or 7."

"All right. Tell me why you think so."

Because you have not previously set objectives in this area, you are going to end up discussing your different opinions of prospecting. Hopefully, this will be resolved during the discussion, and assuming you feel it is an important area, you will come to an agreement on new objectives. But suppose it does not get resolved?

"John, I've explained all the reasons why I don't feel I can rate you any higher in the area of prospecting. Somehow I haven't been able to convince you of its importance, and it doesn't look like you will convince me. Let's set an objective for this area that we can review again in, say, two months. Is that agreeable?"

In the foregoing example, there was a need to compromise. Neither side was close enough to concede agreement. In this instance, Ed, having carefully thought through what he considers appropriate behavior for John, is not in a position to compromise the rating given. However, he is willing to qualify his stand by acknowledging a difference in thinking and jump ahead to setting a specific short-term (even partial) objective, which may eventually open new insight into the disagreement. Ed may compromise with the objectives set, not with the priority he gives to the function.

Discussing Behavior

The activities of the job form the basis for the discussion of what is acceptable behavior. At issue will always be the correct standard for measuring that performance. We noted this in the discussion of prospecting between John and Ed. Often, at the heart of any review will be a discussion centering on behavior—working harder or smarter; spending more, or less, time on; having an attitude toward.

As long as the discussion can center on measurable standards of performance, the manager stays on solid ground. His skill is the skill of questioning. This is an open discussion, not an inquisition. Therefore, the manager must work to keep the channels of communication open. He can do this only through two-way, nondefensive dialog.

You cannot discuss behavior by telling. Your skill is that of reinforcing or clarifying what the salesperson has said. This means using open-ended questions to fully explore the feelings of the other person ("Why would you say that? What would change that? That's an interesting point, go on. Suppose it were just the reverse? What would happen if you did?"). It also means being a good listener. Listen for meaning, not for words. If you can't find the meaning, ask, "Why do you feel that way?"

Behavior, when misunderstood, can be a cause of conflict through the defensive reaction it may provoke. You cannot resolve defensiveness, but the other person can. You defuse the conflict when you let the other person continue to talk. Using open-ended questions will help resolve conflict without your losing your position of authority. Questions help you remain objective, or at least they will enable you to seem objective.

The skills of performance appraisal are simply the skills of being a manager—the sort of skills that make the system work.

Concluding the Discussion

The principle behind any performance review lies in a common acceptance of what the sales job is all about, what is acceptable performance, and how it will be measured. Performance is satisfactory when certain agreed-upon conditions are met.

When all of the discussion has been finished, there remains only the job of setting and agreeing to new objectives to carry forward into the future. The rules are simple. The new objectives

Should be stated in terms of job-related standards.
Should be readily measurable.
Should be attainable.
Should specify a time for review of progress.
Should be mutually agreed-upon.

Finally, the objectives should reflect a need for improvement. Given a situation where performance is outstanding, objectives can express a need "to maintain the status-quo." Few achieve this stage. Where a need for continued growth is paramount, all the objectives should express that need. It is less important that there may be only two or three objectives. It is very important that they are set where standards are not being met.

Setting Standards

One final point. We set standards for the job. We set objectives for people. The standards should be the same for everyone holding that job. Yet performance will vary from individual to individual. For example, a new salesperson's objectives may be less demanding than those of the experienced professional. But the standard of performance will remain the same for all. The standard of performance stays with the job.

A "trainee" may be above the average for all trainees in terms of performance, yet in terms of the job standards, the trainee may be barely average. Anything else means that you have different standards for different levels of experience. You can do this, but it should be clearly understood what the standards are.

"You're Fired!"

I have heard it said that "you cannot fully understand what management means until you have fired your first employee." I would agree with the statement, with the added proviso that there is undoubtedly no more emotional, soul-searching period in a manager's career. Furthermore, there is no "easy" way to do it; there is only a justifiable way.

When do you fire? In essence, when a salesperson continues to turn in a below-average performance record in spite of all attempts to help him improve. When there is a failure to meet reasonable and attainable objectives—objectives that in themselves reflect acceptable standards of performance—then the manager has no further choice if the standards of his own position are going to be met.

None of this will make the decision any less emotional, any less difficult—only necessary. The reasons for the failure should not be at issue—regardless of any such considerations as poor previous selection or lack of experience, and in spite of how hard the salesperson keeps on trying. The decision may only seem tu be subjective. If all the procedures discussed in this chapter have been carried out and there does not appear to be a reasonable chance for that individual to meet the acceptable standards set for sales performance, there is no excuse for continuing to let him fill the position.

You are only delaying the inevitable. In these circumstances, there is only one piece of advice: Do it! There is no other way.

When the decision has been made, the salesman should be told exactly where he stands and the reason for the decision.

> "Ralph, your performance to date has been unacceptable, as we have discussed at length during this review. Here are a series of objectives that we will review again in two months" (or one month or three months). "I want you to clearly understand that your failure to meet these objectives will result in your dismissal. I will be happy to help you in any way. As a matter of fact, let's plan to meet at the end of the month and talk about how you are doing. Ralph, is it absolutely clear what I am asking? Let's look at these objectives again to be sure you understand what must be done."

For the new manager, I would advise discussing the situation with your superior prior to the performance review. In addition, a letter summarizing the reasons for possible dismissal and restating the objectives to be met along with the time frame should be given both to the salesperson involved and to your supervisor.

> Having once dismissed a salesman under the most justifiable conditions, and following the concepts presented in this chapter, I later had the embarrassment of having that salesman issue a completely blown-out-of-proportion account of our review session. A detailed letter in the file of my own manager and possibly that of the personnel department could have prevented this.

That incident happened a number of years ago. With today's legal environment, the wisest course will be an open discussion with both your manager and your personnel department before you take any action. From the point of view of a manager, these precautionary steps are merely procedural. The final action always reflects a management decision.

6

The Case
for Team Building:
What Makes One Group
More Effective Than
Another?

It is not the purpose of sales management to create a happy sales force. The purpose of sales management is to create customers. Although happiness is a great idea, it has never been shown that there is any relationship between happy salespeople and getting business. What, then, should be your goals in managing people?

Not too long ago, I participated in a discussion with a number of business leaders in the Chicago area during which the question came up, "Do salespeople really create sales?"—and in which it became evident that the feeling of the group was a resounding *no*! More important, they felt that the fault was in the lack of management motivation. Thus, they regarded ineffective management as being at the heart of a poor selling effort. The proposition, then, is not "How do you manage?" but, "How do you manage effectively in dealing with your salespeople?"

Management has been popularly defined as "working through others." All of the studies have come to the conclusion that success as a manager is directly related to success in understanding and motivating people: your employees, your peers, your superiors, and—oh, yes—your customers. There is no reason to doubt that your managerial success lies in your success at motivation.

Yet a major reason for managerial failure has also been shown to be not an acceptance of the positive results of effective motivation but rather a miscomprehension regarding the nature of motivation. It comes from a belief about the very nature of people that has been embedded in our business culture—a belief that motivating people is a mechanical problem.

> This statement brings to mind a story about George Westinghouse. It was years before the turn of the century. Westinghouse had just been informed by one of his supervisors that a favorite project was delayed. "Well," said Westinghouse, "I'll just have to hurry over there and motivate them!"

As sales managers, we still continue rushing about with the objective of motivating the sales force. Yet it is interesting that when a salesman fails, it is not we who did not motivate but the salesman who was not motivated.

Some 30 years ago, Douglas McGregor was preaching about Theory X and Theory Y—the conclusion being that the employee was not instinctively lazy and in need of being pushed (Theory-X belief), but self-actualizing if given the chance (Theory-Y belief). Managers listened and said they agreed. But they went right on rushing about "charging up the troops." Perhaps many of them consciously thought they were Theory-Y managers. I like to think they sincerely believed that they wanted to give their employees the chance to be self-directing but that the fault was with the employees. "If McGregor is right, why can't my salesmen make more calls? God knows, I'd give them a chance if they'd just show they could handle it!"

> My stepfather, a self-made executive with the Burlington Railroad, went to the office every Sunday morning "because a number of employees come in on the weekend, and someone has to make sure it's done right, as long as they're going to be there working."

Where is the solution?

All of us, myself and everyone reading these pages at this moment hold preconceived ideas—faulty, perhaps, certainly diverse—but we look at the world with our own unique perspectives. This awareness governs the way we view our salespeople.

We have been developing this moment's awareness all of our lives. We have bred it and then reinforced it very carefully through selective reading, selective listening, selective retention. We have accepted input from our peers, our teachers, our parents and relatives, and the environment we grew up in. They say the first boss we had plays a big role in the instinctive way we now manage, good or bad. By the time we are 18 or 21 years old, we have become pretty fixed in who we are and how we look at what is our private world. Certainly, the potential for continued learning always exists for us, as does the potential for change. But when you have spent some 20 years developing who you are, you are not going to give it up easily.

In this process of growing and developing, we took on a set of attitudes, beliefs, and values about our world and the people in it. We developed attitudes or feelings about a lot of things and the way they ought to be. We developed beliefs about what was true or false in our world. We took some of those attitudes and beliefs and made them a part of our behavior, our value system, which dictates to us what is important.

How we react to a stimulus in our world will depend on something called temperament or personality. For example, given a reason for reacting (a stimulus), our reaction may be quick, direct, and dominant, or it may be weak or passive. We may react by striving to overcome or control whatever threatens us. We may control by influencing others to a favorable reaction or merely by accepting what has happened and striving for harmony at all costs, backing away from a direct confrontation. We call this pattern of reacting our behavior. What we react to will depend on our values.

Dr. Morris Massey, of the University of Colorado Business School, presents a popular seminar entitled, "What You Are Is What You Were When." Consider three of your salesmen, Tom, Dick, and Harry, whose respective ages are 60, 45, and 20. If, as Dr. Massey and others point out, you now regard their most formative years as being the decade of the ages of 10 or 12 to 22, then consider:

Tom, all things being equal (since there is nothing fixed or permanent about individual human nature), relates to the values that come out of growing up in a time of major economic depression; of World War II, when not to be in uniform was something unpatriotic; of college booze parties; and of the sanctity of marriage. Transportation meant crack trains that you set your watch by, and "hot pants" was a condition, not something you wore.

Dick relates to the values established by Korea, rock groups, TV, *Man in the Gray Flannel Suit*, and White's *Organization Man* culture. The airlines offered jet travel coast to coast, trains still ran on time (but barely), gasoline was $0.32 per gallon, and you could buy a new car for around $2,600 (and pay for it with a 4 percent loan).

Harry is a now person. He has never known a period when the country has not been engaged in serious military action somewhere, most of which it has managed to mess up. People do not work for corporations in Harry's world, nor do they have loyalty to their jobs, not if they are "smart." Sticking with one company is too slow a career path. Everyone has or is getting an MBA, and while he himself is not on anything "hard," he has several friends who drop out occasionally. Harry's mother has probably gone back to work just to make ends meet, and only two of his close friends are married, while most of the rest are either divorced or living together or both.

You can do a little arithmetic and think about your own value system. But the point here is that, as a manager, you are going to have to be able to relate to all the Toms, Dicks, and Harrys—all the Carols, Nancys, and Lisas who do not have to understand or relate to you.

There were certain years that forged your management values also. Your "puritan ethic" may have come from a strong role model, whether it still exists or not. A number of the people who managed you (and still do) grew up with a so-called Newton's law of motivation: that people are perceived to be like a physical body at rest—the application of an external force is required to set them in motion, to "motivate" them. Consequently, we have to "get out there and push 'em!" We have to become adept at applying rewards and punishment. We cannot rate an individual too high on the annual review or we will have no way to inspire him to greater progress for the next review.

At every turn, we hear about the "productivity crisis" that has gripped the country. It is difficult to dispute that it exists; the numbers appear substantially correct and even logical. The point is what to do about it, and you can get some good advice from just about everyone, including the "expert" on the third bar stool from the back who has just returned from Japan or Germany or has a friend who did. We read Lester Thurow's *Dangerous Currents* (it's our political and economic policy doing it to us) or Paul Lawrence and David Dyer on *Renewing American Industry* (lack of corporate direction is the culprit). We are in the throes of change. Witness Alvin Toffler's *The Third Wave* (we must be ready to capitalize on the new directions). We have tried quality circles (they don't work fast enough). And throughout, we have the recurring advice that management must learn to motivate its people.

Well, we have learned. As a matter of fact, we have just about fully exploited the possibilities of any further motivation. We have tried giving raises, extra holidays, prizes, and service awards. It is not that these things are not important. They are. But they do not motivate. They may never have. Yet we keep on holding company picnics, assigning spaces in the parking lot, and the like—and because our employees grab for such goodies, we think we are motivating them.

Industry has done a magnificent job of harnessing the physical sciences. We can communicate with anyplace on earth, control nuclear fission, mitigate world starvation (to an extent), and produce a soda can and a plastic trash bag that are indestructible (together with a $15,000 automobile that rusts out two years before it's paid for). We have become masters of the technical world—and have not yet begun to understand people. It is only within the past few years that our psychologists have even come to agree that all people are motivated (in spite of the fact that motivating people is exactly what management has been running around trying to do). This includes that salesman who cannot get his expense account in on time or the fellow who cannot make more than four calls a day. They are all motivated—but people do things for their reasons, not ours. Could we have been playing by the wrong rules?

The test of management is its ability to make common people achieve uncommon performance. People have always been the basic resource of any business organization. People are also the most costly and hardest-to-reproduce resource, and they are the resource that depreciates the quickest when not given enough attention. As any manager knows, it takes time and effort to build an effective sales team, but it can be destroyed in one thoughtless moment.

The Case for Effective Team Building

Fred Kennedy is regional manager for Mebco Equipment Company. His operation effectively covers a 50-mile radius from the Central City office and includes five salesmen, two secretaries, and two planning and layout specialists who share the office space and provide their services to several other regions besides Central City, reporting directly to the manager of marketing services at the factory. Also sharing the office is the regional service manager and his department of 24 installation and service engineers.

Fred has been reviewing negotiations with Tom Plankton, one of his younger salespeople. Fred says, "I'm sorry I had to be downstate just when the Hillman job broke for you. Did you get your bid in as we discussed?" "I made it," replies Tom. "And by the skin of my teeth. I couldn't get ahold of anyone at the factory who could fill in the spec data, for one thing. . . ." Dan breaks in, "What about Ralph here in the office? He's sold so many of those drives he knows more about them than the engineers." "I asked him if he would help, but he said he had to work on another job of his own." Dan didn't say anything, but he knew it was the darn "everyone for himself" attitude around the office. None of the salesmen wanted to take the time to help another out. "I had to estimate the installation figures," Tom continued. "Our illustrious service manager said he was too busy, and the sales department would probably lose it anyway. We just about did. I ended up typing it myself at the last minute. The typists said they had to get their invoices out because it was the end of the accounting period, or something like that."

After Tom left, Fred sat quietly thinking about what had just been said. "It's a good office, with highly capable people," he mused—"except they're all a bunch of individualists going in their own directions instead of pulling together to the same drumbeat. Sometimes I think that I'm the only unifying force in the whole operation. When I leave town, the entire organization just about stops talking to each other. All I seem to do is holler and bang their heads together."

One of Fred's peers is Zack Taylor, the regional manager of another Mebco district. Although both Fred's and Zack's offices are of almost equal size and potential, Zack's operation is continually

outproducing most other districts. About the time Fred was reviewing negotiations with Tom, Zack was deep in a similar discussion
with Ed Holloworth, a salesman. Zack has just asked, "Did you
have any problems getting the Hastings bid off while I was gone last
week?" Ed smiles. "No problems. I did have some trouble finding
any of the application people at the plant, but Dave Flemming said
he would drop what he was doing and give me a hand. We came
pretty close to the wire, and as a matter of fact, you may get some
flack from headquarters accounting when the invoice sheets don't
get finished on time, but we—that is, Dave, Sam Ferguson the service manager, and I—talked to the typists about the importance of
this bid, and they agreed it had to take priority. You should have
seen Sam Ferguson: He was even doing some of the typing himself."
Zack smiled silently to himself. He had worked hard to build just
such a spirit in the district, and it was really paying off. Sometimes
he wondered why they even needed him—unless it was to keep the
factory off their backs.

For many years, it has been accepted that the success or failure
of a business could be directly attributed to the competence of its
management. Until recently, this was understood to mean the expertise of its top management, since this was the source of the corporation's direction and momentum. Lately, we have come to realize that the success or failure of a business lies in the expertise of
the managers at all levels who are responsible for its day-to-day
operation.

In this chapter, we will examine conclusions from a series of
studies of the nature of management team building, quoting specific
references where applicable. In the following chapter, having reviewed the basic concepts and arguments for building an effective
team, we will examine a theory of effective management style.

Studies such as those conducted by Rensis Likert at the University of Michigan (*New Patterns of Management* [New York:
McGraw-Hill, 1961]) show that significantly better or more productive results are obtained by managers such as Zack Taylor, who
have developed their operations into well-knit, effectively functioning teams, as contrasted to managers such as Fred Kennedy, whose
operations are more traditionally managed. This is not to negate
any other statements regarding the importance of the manager's
understanding and dealing with the unique psychological needs of
each employee but rather to propose that total effectiveness lies in

tying the individual members of a department together to form a functioning and supportive team.

A review of other writers—notably Douglas McGregor (*Leadership and Motivation* [Cambridge, Massachusetts: MIT Press, 1966]) and Chris Argyris (*Management and Organizational Development: The Path from XA to YB* [New York: McGraw-Hill, 1971])—shows that Likert's contemporaries agree with his earlier writings, that leadership "is the process of influencing the activities of others in efforts toward goal achievement in given situations."

What we shall see is that this research produces the important conclusion that the managers achieving high productivity are those who have built their departments into operations characterized by cooperative attitudes, high levels of job satisfaction, and loyalty to the group to which the members belong. The research further indicates that tough-acting, technically knowledgeable, task-oriented managers such as Fred Kennedy can also achieve high productivity but that such operations, more often than not, are affected by wasted motion, busywork, and turnover.

In addition, such departments as Fred Kennedy's tend to be one-man operations, with all authority, decisions, and success invested in the supersalesman manager. Studies also show that the improved productivity of such operations does not continue when that specific manager leaves. It is also important to our current discussion to point out that the studies of Likert and his contemporaries were conducted with professional employees and sales groups rather than with factory workers (factories being the more common settings for such studies).

Argyris and McGregor, as well as Saul Gellerman (*Management by Motivation* [New York: AMACOM, 1968]), point out that effective organizational teams are, in effect, functioning social systems, exhibiting high degrees of understanding and sensitivity to others within the group; that in addition, they have good interpersonal skills and a high degree of group loyalty. As a side issue, Argyris indicates that members of such effectively functioning teams are more likely to experience stronger identification with their group, have a greater feeling of belonging to it, have more friends in the group and in the company than outside, show a more favorable job attitude, and express higher productivity goals with more actual productivity and with less sense of pressure or frustration than members of less team-oriented groups.

In other words, there are clear indications that when members of a sales team are united in achieving common goals and supported through the positive attitude of their sales manager, such groups can achieve far more than the same individuals acting separately. This is really what is meant by synergism. Perhaps, also, this is the reason for picnics, and even for sales meetings.

Let me clarify one point before something becomes misunderstood. Data presented later will point out the need for the manager to blend in and adapt his behavior to the temperament and behavioral needs of the sales group. This is not to propose a change in the manager's style, but merely to recognize the need for a flexible style—a style to fit the situation.

The Search for the Ideal

There is evidence to indicate that a single, ideal, or "normal" style of managerial behavior is unrealistic, although an ideal type of leader behavior is commonly considered a goal and is often stressed in management training seminars. One could almost conclude from the stated objectives of such seminars that most managers want to be told how to act. This has been the focal point and reason for the success of the Managerial Grid and other similar "ideal-oriented" training programs, which make as much sense as saying that there is an ideal sales behavior, although Dr. Blake and Dr. Mouton, who created the Managerial Grid® program, have also been successful in selling their Sales Grid® seminar, with the concept of an ideal sales behavior goal. Dr. John Geier of the University of Minnesota notes, "There are no good or bad patterns in behavior; there are only differences in people" (*Emotions of Normal People* [Minneapolis: Persona Press, 1979]). The effective manager or salesman is the one who knows and understands his personal style and uses the individual and unique strengths of that style to interact with others.

What all of the researchers are saying is that the more managers adapt their styles of leadership behavior to meet the particular situation and the needs of their salespeople, the more effective they will tend to be in reaching personal and organizational goals. It is not a matter of the "best" style, but of the most effective style for a particular situation. What is suggested is that a manager's behavioral style may be effective or ineffective, depending on the situation being faced.

According to F. Fiedler (*A Theory of Leadership Effectiveness* [New York: McGraw-Hill, 1967]), three major situational variables determine whether a given situation is favorable to a manager and thus influence the adaptive style he will use. These include, first, the manager's personal relationship with the sales force; second, the degree to which the various salespeople can realistically support each other in the performance of their tasks (for example, a salesman with a territory remote from the others might find it logistically difficult to act in support of another; however, the manager could find other means to promote such support—say, by having the sales force give technical support to each other); and third, the power and authority that the manager's position holds in relation to those group members who may not report directly to him.

> Referring to the previous case of Mebco, the planning and layout specialists as effective team members report to the division marketing services manager. To what degree does the regional manager's title carry an implied authority over these members? Thus, different management situations may require different managerial styles.

As noted earlier, this does not imply that a manager should strive to change his basic instinctive behavior pattern but that the manager should be willing to adopt a more flexible behavior to meet different situations. Fiedler confirms that a manager's style often reflects his personally developed motivational and need structure and that even should the manager desire it, it would take two or three years of intense psychotherapy to effect a lasting basic change in his personality structure. We have spent too many years and expended too much effort on developing the personality we have to change easily. Thus, the success of organizational development depends on the individual manager's being able to diagnose and understand his own temperament and leadership style, not on his ability to change that style for another, even an ideal one.

While supporting the earlier work of Fiedler, Robert J. House (*A Path-Goal Theory of Leader Effectiveness* [Carbondale, Illinois: Southern Illinois University Press, 1974]) concluded in his studies that "the most effective leader behavior style is one that is high on supportive behavior, and low on task behavior." John Stinson and

Thomas Johnson ("The Path-Goal Theory of Leadership: Suggested Refinement," *Management Journal* [June 1975]) suggest that the relationship is more complex and that the amount of task behavior should depend on the needs of the followers as well as the type of task the followers are performing. (Hold onto this thought. It is very important to where we are heading.)

This principle of a "supportive relationship" on the part of management contains within it an important clue to its effective application. What the researchers are saying is that the manager must take into consideration the experience and expectations of each member of his "team." To do this, the sales manager needs to know how the salespeople view their world and understand each one's behavioral personality. Further, the manager needs to accurately assess how his own behavioral characteristics will be received by the sales force.

These conclusions agree with the previously mentioned work of Likert at the Institute for Social Research at the University of Michigan. Under the guidance of Likert, the institute conducted an intensive study program aimed at a better understanding of the human aspects of managing and the effects of the complexity of human behavior on these aspects. In summary, the study showed that those managers who concentrated on the individual personality of each of their salespeople had the best performance records and that those managers tended to instill within their salespeople a spirit of working toward the common high performance goals of the district or region. It showed that these achieving managers were "employee-centered" rather than "job-centered"—people-oriented rather than task-oriented, at least in their outward appearance, if not in their basic temperament profiles.

Putting the Theory to Work

Classical management theory, such as Douglas McGregor's Theory X, emphasizes that the particular job and work style of the typical salesman must be clearly specified and closely supervised. Implicit in such a belief is the idea that salesmen cannot be trusted to do a full day's work, that they will abuse any freedom given them by "goofing off," or that they will at least work in an ineffective manner if left to their own devices.

An example of the result of such management thinking can be taken from the use made of the familiar sales call report. Unfortunately, the call report too often degenerates into another method of forcing predetermined work behavior patterns upon the sales force, which is the result of Theory-X thinking. Where the call report is used as a communication device between manager and salesman, and as a planning and scheduling aid for more effective territory coverage, it then becomes a part of the professional manager's effective tools, which is Theory-Y thinking.

With such Theory-Y thinking, you would suppose that salespeople would feel more free to set their own work patterns and would thus be more productive. This unfortunately does not hold true as a general observation. The University of Michigan studies by Likert referred to earlier have shown that this freedom to act is effective only in situations in which there is also a high degree of interpersonal interaction among members of the sales force as individuals and between the sales force as a group and their manager. That is, if freedom to act independently is to contribute to high performance, the individual must be a part of an organizational group where there is frequent interplay, contact, and interaction among the membership of that group as well as with the sales manager. Where the individual has the skills needed as well as the high performance goals and motivation arising from such group interaction, then being given the freedom to act will result in improved and effective performance, and the individual will be motivated to higher productivity. Freedom for group members to act on their own does not necessarily result in high performance. It is a team phenomenon.

Thus, only when every salesperson in your organization contributes to an effectively functioning team that has a high degree of group loyalty and effective group interaction and meets your set performance goals can you say that you are making full use of all potential capabilities that are available to you. Team building is not a program, but an objective of your management function.

The Effect of Group Maturity

Chris Argyris has stated that the maturity of the group in terms of its members' "working together" (that is, maturity not in terms of age, but in terms of experience) has an important bearing on the manager's style in dealing with them. As the group, working together as a team, continues to grow in terms of accomplishing regional objectives, the manager should consciously move away from task-oriented behavior and increase his relationship behavior. Then, as the group continues to increase in maturity in terms of its members' supportive team effort, the manager can decrease both task and relationship behavior, since group members will provide their reinforcement. At this stage, we can say that the involvement of the manager is literally not necessary for continued support. The group becomes self-actualizing, which further supports the group's maturity through the manager's trust and confidence. Harold Geneen, chairman of ITT Corporation, once said, "The most difficult task of the leader is to know when to grab the tiller as the first mate steers the ship into the rocks without destroying the self-confidence of the mate" (perhaps a "never-never land," but certainly a desirable goal).

D. C. Pelz (*Motivation of the Engineer* [New York: American Management Association, General Management Series, 1957]) has reported in substantiating research that it is when the manager's support comes from an understanding of the behavior of others that such knowledge allows the support to be timed in a way that reinforces the salesman's motivation to achieve his most effective performance. In a word, study human nature.

In more and more instances, such research into effective organization has shown that the manager's skill in interacting with his salespeople is an important ingredient in their joining together in a team effort—an effort in which they support each other. Such research also shows that the greater the manager's skill at interpersonal relations and the use of team-building methods, the greater the productivity and the greater the overall job satisfactions of the members of his organizational unit.

Joe Masterson leads a group of six salesmen spread over ten states. The other day, Laura, the Detroit representative, called to discuss a problem she was having. During their discussion, Joe suggested she also contact Bill Perkins in the Milwaukee office, who had had some similar experiences. In a later phone conversation with Perkins, Joe told him of Laura's problem and that she would be calling him. Joe is building a team reliance among his sales group. Although it would have been easy for Joe to have answered Laura directly, that would have reinforced the traditional salesman-manager relationship rather than a supportive team relationship, which builds the spirit of the organization.

Tom Hadley has a similar organizational setup with his sales-people covering far-flung areas. Tom encourages them to communicate regularly with each other by passing articles back and forth, sending each other copies of their memos, and holding quarterly district sales meetings where his sales group can talk over common areas of interest and problems on a face-to-face basis.

Team Building

Beginning in the late 1950s, personnel psychologists and trainers started implementing the ideas of participative management by using such techniques as directed discussion through peer groups, thereby enabling managers to experience group problem solving and share their feelings and emotions in a group climate. Peer discussion can be effective in changing behavior. Holding frequent group meetings with open discussion, given a receptive attitude on the part of the manager toward the ideas and expressions of those in the meeting, can have a positive effect on the attitude of the members of such a group. Unfortunately, studies indicate that unless the manager is sincerely and genuinely interested in the thoughts and feelings of the group and is prepared to act upon their ideas in a totally supportive manner, he is better off not having group meetings to discuss work-related problems or solutions.

The team-building effort presents a complex problem in interrelationships. This complexity of the team-building effort was first observed during World War II, when it was noted that certain leaders were more effective in creating an emotionally positive group effort than others (the Patton charisma). It was first observed in bomber and tank crews who worked closely together.

> Take, for instance, a bomber crew of some seven men under the leadership of their pilot. They slept together, ate together, drank together. And when the leader-pilot said, "Let's go!" they gave a spirited yell and went. Then one day the pilot of such a crew would be gone, and the copilot would assume his place as the new leader. Same group, basically. They would still go into town and drink together, but now when the new leader said, "Let's go!" they went, but there was no longer any spirit in it.

Even though a sales manager might strive to build a team effort with the previous principles in mind, he might not achieve the desired effectiveness because of the interpersonal complexity of such a situation. Yet you have to try. Management is a relative process. For managers to communicate as effectively as they intend, they must be prepared to adapt their specific behavior to take into account its effect on the behavior, expectations, and values of those salespeople with whom they are interacting. Managers are not asked to change their instinctive behavior style but to modify that style to blend with the strengths and job maturity of their particular sales force.

The behavior of the manager alone does not determine how the sales group will respond. Their reaction always depends upon the way they perceive the manager's behavior—that is, what they feel is meant by the actions of their manager.

Every corporation exhibits a distinctive management style—a culture unique to that company. Yet more often than not, the leadership style of the individual manager dominates the department. The manager creates the world of the sales force. From the individual departments comes the effective, as well as the ineffective, managerial unit. The manager's style causes the sales force to be effective in terms of the results they achieve.

Two Systems—Two Directions

Likert identified two distinct systems of management organization (as opposed to the unique styles of individual managers). These systems he referred to as:

The job-related system
The cooperative-motivation system

Likert's job-related system is typified by the so-called scientific management method and is often used effectively in departments where repetitive work is predominant. Herein, jobs are well defined, documented, and organized; wasted motion and inefficient activities are identified and can be kept to a minimum; standards are usually well established for all tasks; and inflexible budgets and tight controls are the existing pattern.

I was discussing management techniques with the national sales manager for a clinical laboratory chain. He was responsible for a group of some ten regionally located laboratories selling blood-analysis services to physicians. Each lab was staffed with a sales manager and some five to eight sales representatives. I asked him, "How much time does your typical sales manager spend in the field with his salespeople?"

"In the case of new people, it will vary with how fast they pick up our way of doing things. We train them very intensively in the first few days to make their presentations the way we want them to. After they are experienced, they should be able to make their own presentations following our guidelines. The managers are not there to close orders. They are there to make sure the salespeople follow the book. That's the whole job of sales managers—to keep their sales force humping!"

"That doesn't leave the salespeople much flexibility to make decisions."

"Salesmen in this company don't need flexibility. What's so difficult about their job? If they leave home on time every morning, follow a route O.K.'d by their managers, and make their prescribed number of calls, then they are doing what they are paid to do, and the sales will follow."

Interestingly, this national sales manager's people do achieve their sales quotas, although turnover is high. But happiness, as we said earlier, is not the goal—sales are. It is difficult to argue with success. Yet here was a sales force plagued with high turnover, low morale, and little self-motivation. It might have been easier for the sales manager to drive his sales force, but how much greater could the productivity have been with a different style? Apparently, his top management also thought there was more to be achieved, since the last I heard, he had been replaced.

In the cooperative-motivation system, work is viewed as being more variable. Performance appears to be achieved more from enthusiasm and a high level of motivation than from "tight" job controls. The cooperative-motivation system depends for its success on the effective use of all areas of motivation—economic as well as the ego motives of belonging, self-esteem, and self-actualization.

For the cooperative-motivation system to work, it needs managers who are skilled in the use of interpersonal relationships, who understand the personal needs of those who work for them. Such managers tend to avoid practices that may, for a time, increase productivity but that eventually tend to affect attitudes adversely and thus ultimately have a less than positive effect on productivity. Any practice or procedure must give the promise of improving both attitude (personal motivation) and productivity, since this is one of their goals as managers.

The Competitive Edge

In summary, all of the research suggests that the amount of influence sales managers have on their departments is related not only to the external authority delegated to them by their superiors but also to the managerial, leadership, or motivational practices and style they use. It suggests, too, that the managers' behavioral style—and the extent to which they effectively use that style to develop a well-knit, loyal, and communicating sales group—is really what establishes the amount of actual authority they have over their people. There also appears to be a direct relationship between this and how much actual influence managers have upward in the organizations with their superiors.

Thus, managers of highly productive operations build a different kind of management system than that found in operations with lower productivity. These different systems, while giving the sales force more influence on their individual operations, also give those managers more influence within their corporations.

Interestingly, the greater the amount of "unreasonable" pressure salespeople feel from their upper management for better performance, the less influence they see their own manager as having with the organizational hierarchy. It is also interesting to note that managers of high-productivity departments appear adept at acting as a "buffer" against the pressures of higher management upon their groups.

The Communications Effect

D. C. Pelz ("Influence: A Key to Effective Leadership," *Personnel* magazine [November 1965]) reports that there are times when even sincere and honest recognition for a "job well done" can have a negative effect on morale. A manager giving such recognition to a group whose morale is already low—where the group exhibits low self-esteem—can find his effort backfiring.

This finding led to an attempt to determine possible reasons for such behavior. As a result, it was confirmed that where there is a difference between what a manager reports (or thinks) he does and the manager's actual behavior as seen by the sales force, such differences in perception often depend more on the past experiences of the salespeople than on anything else—that is, on the expectations, norms, and values of the individual salespeople. In other words, a lack of understanding (miscommunication) results from a difference in perception. As the manager passes on a compliment for an accomplishment, the salesperson would feel no emotional uplift from such praise, since he would feel the praise was not justified, and was given for the manager's own reasons.

In addition, these perceptions on the part of the salespeople also depend on the personality of the manager—that is, on his or her behavioral style. When a manager behaves in ways that do not fit his or her personality, the manager's resultant behavior is apt to communicate something different from what was intended. In other words, any attempt on the part of the manager to modify or blend his or her behavior to meet the needs of the sales force must come from a sincere desire to meet those needs and from an understanding of the results to be achieved. You cannot stage-manage an effective behavioral style.

What all this leads up to is that the high-producing managers have developed their sales organizations into highly coordinated, highly motivated, cooperative social systems. They have accomplished this by treating their salespeople as distinct individuals, understanding their unique differences, strengths, and weaknesses.

Your salespeople all want appreciation, recognition, influence, a feeling of accomplishment, and a feeling that those who are important to them—the manager included—believe in them and respect them. They want to play on a winning team.

The material presented in this chapter represents a summation of what the best minds in industry are thinking and writing concerning why some managers and their organizational units are more productive than others. In the next chapter, we will build on these principles and concepts to present ways in which the new sales manager can put them to work in developing an effective sales team.

7

Developing Your Management Style: How Can I Motivate My Sales Force?

Management has been compared at various times to warfare and to sports events; at other times, to a game. The comparisons are amusing but seldom appropriate. If managing could be confined to a number of prescribed rules, then the skills of the trade would be a lot easier to master. But in the final analysis, management is a human endeavor, strongly influenced by the personality, vision, and leadership ability of one person—the manager—and bearing, for better or worse, the stamp of his personal style.

And what is style? It is a matter of how one expresses oneself. Whether distinctive or mundane, it represents a characteristic approach—in essence, a manner of reacting.

A manager's style can induce or inhibit change. Often the new manager represents change—just by being new. The idea of change in itself can be stimulating. It can bring both people and ideas out of the dustbin of "the way we've always done it." Yet new managers can quickly lose whatever advantage their change promises, depending on their style. Whether that style is good or bad will be decided in the future. For the present, we will content ourselves with the basic concept of style as it exists. Now let's see what you can do with it that is positive.

The best tactic for creating an environment that encourages change in your newly acquired sales organization is to set a personal example. To motivate your salespeople to make a special effort, you have to make a special effort. To encourage them to work harder, you have to work harder than you expect of them. To stimulate them to come up with ideas, you have to come up with ideas. By making sure they see you striving for their success, and by constantly hearing you talk about what success is, they begin to copy your example. Perhaps style, however, is easier to see than to describe.

> As a boss, W.J.D. was seen by many as a charismatic, forceful, driving, dynamic leader. "He could charm the shirt off your back to get what he wanted." Some said he had a style that was magnetic. Yet there were those who found him a tyrant who would sell his grandmother to make a buck. He was feared by those who got in his way. Some said he had a pirate's mentality.

An organization has style, although we tend to see it as "culture." A salesman has style. We are all acquainted with the "flashy" salesman, the "quiet" salesman, the "persistent" salesman. We talk about their "style" of selling.

Just so, every manager has a style—a behavior pattern that each tends to use more or less consistently when dealing with the sales force. Since we know there are differences in managerial styles, the question is thus raised, "What is an effective style?" or, "Is there an effective style?" Jumping ahead, what I hope to show you in this chapter is that effectiveness in a manager results from using a behaviorial style that varies in response to a changing environment. The key to being an effective manager is learning to interpret that environment.

Behavior: Setting the Scene

As a salesman, it did not take any amount of deep thinking for me to realize there was a direct relationship between my successes and good interpersonal relations with my customers. This, in turn, led to the realization that if I were to meet my goals of professionalism,

I was going to have to learn as much as a layman could master about what made one individual react favorably or unfavorably to another. In other words, I was going to have to consider the psychology of behavior.

The task could have presented a number of almost insurmountable obstacles to a busy salesman. There were an immense number of books covering an apparently wide range of differing theories. In other words, where do you start? Fortunately, as manager of sales training for Westinghouse, I was able to turn to the psychology department at the University of Pittsburgh and ask for help. From these early efforts came the material first presented in corporate sales training seminars and later, following further study, in the training workshops I presented as a training consultant, seminar leader, and sales manager.

The behavioral studies on which this training, as well as the material presented in this chapter, is based are used extensively throughout the corporate training world. Based on the early behavioral theories of the Greek philosophers as well as on the clinical work of Dr. William Marston during the 1930s, the theory has in turn formed the basis for the work of Dr. Blake and Dr. Mouton in the presentation of their Managerial Grid® and Sales Grid® seminars, as well as the work of Psychological Associates of St. Louis; Dr. David Merrill of Tracom Corporation in Denver; Dr. John Geier and Performax International in Minneapolis; and a great number of psychologists, consultants, and trainers, including those giving presentations at American Management Association programs.

The Four Temperaments

All of us view the world around us from the vantage point of our own picture window, with our own perception of what that world is. From everything that has been a part of our environment, as well as the experiences we have had throughout our life, we have developed our current awareness of our world.

The experiences of our past life—our playmates, teachers, parents, relatives, everyone—were the raw materials from which we developed our attitudes and our beliefs. From these came our values—those life orientations that tell us what is important to us.

They set the stage for what we will react to and how strong that reaction will be.

We are all creatures of need. Although these needs can vary from time to time and even from moment to moment, we continue to experience, at any given point, one major—at times perhaps overpowering—need. This is felt as tension. We react. What we react to is a part of our value system. How we manifest that reaction is the expression of our behavior. We are all different, but we each tend to react in generally consistent patterns. Thus, our style tends to be instinctively consistent and even predictable.

In working for the growth, productivity, and effectiveness of your sales force, it is important to understand something about their value system—where they are coming from. Equally important is to understand the nature of their behavior system—how they will react. Understanding their behavior aids in understanding how to create the motivational environment that is the manager's role in developing effectiveness.

Dr. John Geier, building on the clinical writings of Dr. William Marston, has cataloged the reactions of individuals to a stimulus (*Emotions of Normal People* [Minneapolis: Persona Press, 1979]), as falling into four quadrants, which he has designated "dominant," "influencing," "steadiness," and "conscientiousness" (shortened to high "D," high "I," high "S," and high "C"), just to assign these concepts a standardized terminology under which they could be studied and recognized and put to use in the field.

The idea of using a grid to chart psychological factors has been attractive to behavioral writers for many years. Because it is so simple, there is a tendency to view the analysis as too rigid. Many who explain human behavior on a layman's level describe the "ten types of buyers" as if this were all there is to it. The fact is that people are much more complex.

A behavioral grid, therefore, is only a teaching tool—a method of explaining. It is not my intent to do more than introduce a bare outline of the theory to learn how individual behavioral tendencies relate to management style.

The concept of the four basic temperaments is useful for several purposes. A person's overall behavior can be described as belonging, more or less, in one of the four categories. Or each category can be used as a scale on which to rate one dimension of a person's behavior separately, and the four dimensions can then be combined for a more detailed composite picture of a personality. Finally, the four temperaments correspond fairly closely to four managerial approaches appropriate with employees of different levels of maturity. In this chapter we'll explore all these ideas as they relate to a sales manager's understanding of his or her sales force. Let's start by using the temperament theory to analyze how four types of salesmen react to the same change in a work situation.

In the temperament theory, behavior is seen as a varying spectrum of reactions to a stimulus. Given the stimulus, reaction will be either quick, direct, and aggressive or slow-building and passive. In addition, the reaction is seen either as long-lasting and presenting a "hostile" or unfavorable environment or as warm, friendly, and favorable and of short duration, quickly fading. These polar definitions form the basis of the theory, which can then be used to characterize the different reactions to whatever stimulus prompted the response in the first place (see Figure 16). The theory becomes a response to the question, "Given an individual whose predominant temperament would fall into this quadrant—how would you describe this person's behavior? What adjectives would you use in doing so?"

Let's see how this theory would apply through several examples.

The High-"D" Temperament

A reorganization in the customer service department has resulted in a number of procedural changes that have affected the response time to the sales force's inquiries and caused some problems with customer calls.

The minute he heard about the changes, David was incensed—willing to tell anyone who would listen what was wrong with the new system and why it wouldn't work. Not that David was opposed to change. There were a number of things he felt were wrong with the old system, and he had cornered several staff managers at the last sales meeting to tell them what he thought should be done. You remember having urged him to write a letter during one of his outbursts, and it took him a month to find the time. Finally, he got around to it, although he would have preferred a face-to-face confrontation, since David is a more direct-acting personality. Feelings stay emotionally strong a long time with him.

Figure 16. The four temperaments.

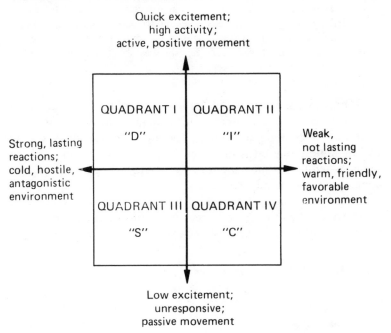

High-"D" personalities fear the loss of control in any situation that they feel is important. Ego-oriented, they seem to resent being told what to do, preferring to "make their own policy" as the occasion seems to them to demand. Having a very direct, driving temperament, the high-"D" individuals are also motivated by an atmosphere of directness—as long as they feel they are basically in control of their environment. Put another way, your directness in dealing with the high-"D" salesman should not appear to be demanding.

David is a good salesman. His enthusiasm, drive, and "Let's do it" temperament have a positive effect on his customers.

The High-"I" Temperament

Irene also had a few derogatory remarks about the new customer service system from the first moment she heard it announced.

However, within minutes she calmed down, her reaction seeming to cool off as quickly as it had flared up. Anyway, the first time Irene needed something from the customer service department, she found she could maintain her control of the interaction through the influence of her personality, and she felt she was able to stay in control of the situation in this manner.

Outgoing, gregarious, and talkative, the high-"I" individuals control through social interaction, through influencing others to their way of thinking and acting. The high-"I" individuals do not like to stand alone on issues, even when they feel strongly about them. When Irene found she was one of the few opposing the new system, she quickly adapted to it.

Irene is a good salesman. Her one difficulty is in pushing for a close, which she rationalizes as not being timely. She prefers to influence rather than dominate a decision by force of will.

The High-"S" Temperament

Shirley took the announcement about the customer service reorganization without comment. Even those first few times when she did not seem to be getting the response she wanted, it did not appear to upset her outwardly. Although she had a few things to say about what she didn't like when it happened the fourth time, she remained reasonably calm even then. It was evident in talking to her that there were points she did not agree with, but throughout, she went out of her way to support the company viewpoint. Things that did bother her continued to do so a long time after the incidents were over.

High-"S" individuals fear change, since change from any established pattern represents insecurity, a loss of the known. They are motivated by the security of settled affairs, by the traditional way of doing things. They can accept change, but they want to know the reasons for the change and would prefer that any change were tried successfully somewhere else before affecting them. Policy, long-standing ways of doing things, standard procedures—all represent security. The high "S" prefers going "by the book."

Shirley is a good salesman. Her customers remain very loyal and often state how much they rely on her steadiness.

The High-"C" Treatment

Charlie seemed concerned that the new customer service policy would disrupt the harmony that he had been able to build between his accounts and the customer service group. While he said it made him nervous, it was not evident in his actions. He went out of his way to explain how the change would help each customer, although it was apparent he did not believe that fully himself. When something did go wrong, he did not let it bother him for very long. His reaction did not last.

The high "C" is extremely conscientious about being sure everything is right and proper. This maintains a harmonious relationship because everyone knows what the rules are and is playing by them.

Charlie is a good salesman. His fear is of disrupting the harmony of a situation or having something not be done the proper way. He is motivated by an environment of "many and very detailed explanations." Being overly involved in the accuracy of doing something the right way, Charlie often becomes a "nitpicker."

These brief character sketches help to introduce the differences in human behavior. You will have noted that each of these individuals is a good salesperson, in his or her own way. The point to remember when you work with the behavioral traits of others is that their patterns are neither effective nor ineffective; they are merely reacting differently.

Granted, in certain circumstances, one type of behavior pattern will be more effective than another, but that is more a matter of being able to adapt one's inherent pattern to meet another person's with a different pattern. You do that constantly in selling. We do it instinctively, perhaps without knowing the basics of the opposing behavior pattern we are adapting to. Dr. David Merrill of Tracon Corporation refers to this as having a dimension of flexibility in behavior reaction.

If I were a high-"D" manager dealing with a salesman with a different behavior pattern from my own, my effectiveness in interpersonal relations would be directly proportionate to my ability to understand my own behavior pattern as well as that of the salesman, and then adapt or modify my behavior to create the most effective environment in which to communicate with and motivate that salesman. Most of us, fortunately, do that pretty successfully by instinct. You have probably been doing that with your customers, as noted. However, even if you have the best of intentions, instinct alone is not always enough when you strive to be a better salesman—or a better manager.

Up to this point, we have tended to speak of individual behavior patterns as being totally high-"D," high-"I," or whatever. This is not completely accurate, since every one of us has each of these temperaments to a certain extent within our total pattern, with each temperament modifying the others to some degree. Thus, another means of looking at behavior is to consider each of the four dimensions of behavior as existing on a different relative scale, higher or lower than some norm for that particular dimension. Using such an approach, the four dimensions of behavior would look like this:

"D" (dominance): An approach to obtaining results
> High "D"—Tends to take an active, assertive, direct approach to getting results.
> Low "D"— Tends to obtain results through a more organized, deliberate, calculated approach.

"I" (influencing): An approach to interacting with others
> High "I"— Tends to approach other people in an open, outgoing, gregarious manner. Tends emotionally to be impulsive.
> Low "I"— Tends to approach other people in a more controlled, reserved manner. Strongly controls emotions.

"S" (steadiness): An approach to social or work environment
> High "S"— Tends to prefer a controlled, predictable environment established with standards of behavior.
> Low "S"— Tends to prefer a more unstructured, flexible environment without restrictions.

"C" (conscientiousness): Adherence to established standards
> High "C"—Tends to prefer things being done the "right way"—by the book.
> Low "C"— Tends to see the right way as being his way, where

the "right way" is carefully defined according to his own terms.

If we could now plot each temperament on some relative scale along each of these four dimensions, we would have pictorially graphed our "pattern" (see Figure 17). What is interesting to us as laymen is that most of us have one or at most two predominating behavior dimensions to our patterns. Thus, for all intents and purposes, we can speak and work with others, our customers and our salesmen, as if each had in reality a single dominant temperament.

As managers, we operate in rather complicated social systems in which we have three levels of need thrust upon us: (1) the need to understand why people behave as they do, (2) the need to predict how people will react in a specific situation, and (3) the need to be able to have a positive impact on the behavior of others. We control our impact on others through an understanding of the effects of style.

Some Elements of Behavior

To help you more clearly understand how style contributes to effective management, we must look briefly at some of the work that has been done in the ever expanding arena of organizational behavior.

Modern research of the so-called motivating environment can trace their beginnings to the early Hawthorne studies. These efforts were undertaken by Elton Mayo and his associates in the early 1920s at the Hawthorne, Illinois, plant of the Western Electric Company. The researchers were attempting to study the effect of illumination on productivity. What happened was that everything they did seemed to increase efficiency. What they were observing, it was determined later, was not the effect of the change in illumination, but the effect of the attention that was being given to the people studied. These early observations later came to be known as the "Hawthorne effect." Namely, people responded to the effort to make them stand out. They felt important. They felt a part of something happening around them.

The next notable step came in the early 1950s, with the formulation of the now-famous Theory-X/Theory-Y pronouncements

Figure 17. Four Behavior Dimensions.

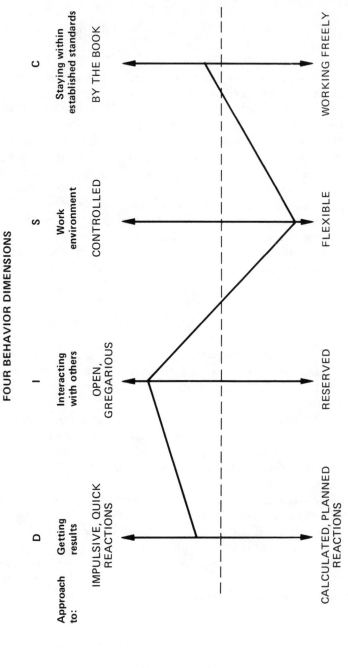

FOUR BEHAVIOR DIMENSIONS

	D	I	S	C
Approach to:	Getting results	Interacting with others	Work environment	Staying within established standards

IMPULSIVE, QUICK REACTIONS

OPEN, GREGARIOUS

CONTROLLED

BY THE BOOK

CALCULATED, PLANNED REACTIONS

RESERVED

FLEXIBLE

WORKING FREELY

of Douglas McGregor, which we touched on briefly in the previous chapter. McGregor theorized that management thinking could be polarized into two groups. Theory X represented the then-typical viewpoint that workers were inherently lazy, that they had to be driven and closely supervised, that motivation came only on a "carrot-and-stick" level. As the opposite, he proposed Theory-Y thinking: that workers wanted to achieve, that they were basically self-directed if given the opportunity and shown the way. Perhaps McGregor's greatest contribution was his promotion of the idea that management needed a more accurate understanding of human nature and the nature of motivation.

Even while management accepted the logic of McGregor's theories, little happened. Management conceded the need to move to Theory Y but continued to manage with Theory X principles. Perhaps managers weren't ready to take the step—even though they acknowledged the need for change.

In the 1960s, Chris Argyris of Harvard offered an expanded version of McGregor's work by integrating two different behavior patterns (Type A and Type B) along with Theory-X and Theory-Y assumptions. The pattern-A type of behavior was nonsupportive of others, did not own up to feeling emotional about others, and was physically dominating, directing, and controlling through the power of position or strength. Pattern-B behavior, on the other hand, was open, supportive of others, and willing to give the other person the benefit of the doubt. Thus, management thinking and management behavior were presented as separate elements of a basic problem.

According to Argyris, there exists a progression from XA to YB, with a predictable path of growth that contributes to getting there. Thus, growth in management relationships moves from XA, in which negative people assumptions are coupled with nonsupportive behavior, to XB, in which there are still negative people assumptions but behavior is supportive. (An analogy might be the tough bosses whom everyone respects for what they accomplish with those who can put up with them.) Growth then moves to YA, where management thinks that people are self-actualizing but still need close supervision. The final step is to YB, with supportive behavior matched with positive people assumptions on the part of the manager.

What is important for us in the Argyris studies is the effect that he found on differing management practices as the managers develop in maturity in their jobs. Argyris contended that worker apathy and apparent laziness were not inherent personality problems but rather the result of the workers' being kept from developing by the strictly controlled supervisory practices still dominant in industry.

In the ensuing years, David McClelland of Harvard added to these findings through his research on achievement motivation, discovering that maturity (in terms of education and experience) in a given situation was a determining factor in achieving a desired result. Thus, as we will see, managers should vary their task and people relationship ratio depending on the maturity of the individual or group involved. (Today, only a short time span of ten or so years later, we find workers in "automated" plants also taking responsibility for fixing the machines they tend.)

Following Argyris's thinking consider the work of Frederick Herzberg and his associates at the Psychological Service of Pittsburgh, whose studies involved hundreds of engineers and other professionals. Herzberg concluded that people have two categories of need, which affect their behavior in different ways.

The first need category Herzberg called "hygiene factors," because they have to do with our work environment. These are not really part of the job, but they have an effect on the conditions under which the work is performed. They would include such factors as administrative policies, type of supervision, working conditions, money, status, security, the subsidized cafeteria, and the assigned parking space or the type of company car. "Hygiene factors" do not increase productivity; they merely prevent loss. They make people comfortable in their jobs. The second need category Herzberg called "motivators." These were factors that affect the workers' feelings of achievement, professional growth, recognition, and increased responsibility.

Developing Theory into Style

Then came Rensis Likert and his colleagues at the University of Michigan, whose work implemented the previous studies of McGregor, Argyris, Herzberg, and others in the field through organizational training programs in numerous industrial settings. Likert's work, together with the expanded work of Paul Hersey and Kenneth Blanchard at Ohio University, organized management styles into a behavior relationship grid, shown in Figure 18. Note that the four management styles in this grid correspond approximately to

Figure 18. Relationship between manager behavior and employee maturity.

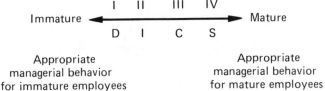

II	III
High-task, high-people approach	Low-task, high-people approach
(Easiest for high "I" managers)	(Easiest for high "C" managers)
I	IV
High-task, low-people approach	Low-task, low-people approach
(Easiest for high "D" managers)	(Easiest for high "S" managers)

```
                      I    II   III   IV
        Immature  ◄─────────────────────►  Mature
                      D    I    C     S
```

| Appropriate managerial behavior for immature employees | Appropriate managerial behavior for mature employees |

the four temperaments mentioned earlier. If you turn the grid in Figure 18 ninety degrees clockwise, you'll see how the letters line up with those in Figure 16 (although the quadrant numbers don't align).

Such studies have categorized the outward appearances of different managerial behavior into a continuum of four distinct approaches. In quadrant I, the manager's behavior is seen as emphasizing the work, the task to be accomplished, while seemingly ignoring the interpersonal aspects of the job—in other words, setting tight task rules with little freedom for personal initiative. In terms of behavior reaction, this type of style would be represented by the high-"D" temperament: direct, dominant, total control.

In quadrant II, management style moves to a seemingly higher level of people awareness, but task control remains firmly in place. As an analogy, we might say that since the people are approaching the task in the manner prescribed by the manager, the manager can let them set their own pace. This is the personality style most closely associated with the high-"I" temperament: direction by influence.

A quadrant-III management profile is seen as trusting people implicitly and knowing that the apparent lack of forceful task emphasis will not be misunderstood. High-"C" behavior is most representative of a managerial style falling in this area.

Quadrant IV would be represented by the high-"S" personality, with its nonsupportive behavior. As a managerial style, this would be seen as turning over all direction to the employees to proceed with the performance of their tasks as they perceive to be proper (assuming, of course, their understanding and acceptance of established company policy and the policy directives of the manager). With truly mature, experienced professional salespeople, this could indeed be the proper choice, as we shall see.

One important aspect of these patterns must be noted: These are the basic managerial behavior styles *as they are seen by others*, not solely or necessarily as the manager intends them to be perceived.

Appropriate Managerial Style

As the results of the various studies were brought together in the workplace, it became evident that what was being proposed had little about it in the way of sustaining effectiveness. Success, it was recognized, has to do with how the individual or the group behaves. In other words, we reward what we consider proper behavior. Effectiveness, on the other hand, depends on the attitude with which the individual or group behaves. I may outwardly react properly toward the situation but if my attitude is negative I stand less of a chance of being effective. Such factors can be expressed in a way that is analogous to "force-field analysis," as sketched in the top half of Figure 19, and as it relates to the situation that follows.

> Ed, the sales manager we met in Chapter 5, has a personal goal that diverges slightly from that of the corporation when it comes to the issue of John's prospecting effort. The corporate goal is for John to be on target with his sales volume. Thus, while Ed could be arguing that better prospecting techniques would contribute to corporate goals, let's assume that in reality Ed's insistence stems more from his attitude that prospecting activity, being a part of all sales jobs, must therefore be included in John's duties. It makes Ed look better with his superior if his salespeople are performing all functions of the job.
>
> John's goals, on the other hand, do not include prospecting and thus are represented as being in opposition to Ed's goals. John's attitude is one of hostility to the issue at hand. Therefore, the result, as seen in the force-field graph of Figure 19, is that John's prospecting will not contribute its full share to the overall company goal.

Thus, the relationship between the salesman's and manager's goals determines the extent to which the company's goals are achieved. The lesson to be learned from the above situation is twofold: The manager, in every instance, represents the driving force, the motivating environment. The salesperson represents the restraining force, that being acted on. The factors that divert the salesperson's effort from the company or district goal are attitudinal expressions of hostility to an idea, to the manager himself, to working conditions that are regarded as being poor, to policies of the company or the manager, to procedures—even to the type of car the salesperson drives.

What we are searching for is the appropriate management style that will bring the salesman's effort more closely in line with company objectives. This implies a possible attitude change on the part of both the manager and the salesman. In other words, this may involve the managers' being more cognizant of their own be-

Figure 19. Behavior results expressed as interdependent forces.

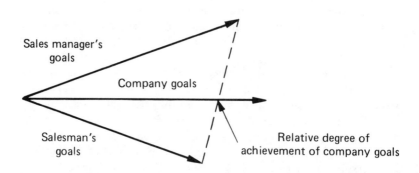

havior as well as the behavior of the salesmen, in keeping with overall company objectives, and more effectively directing the needed changes in the objectives of the salesmen. (Incidentally, this is also what management by objectives is all about.)

Back to the case of Ed and John: If Ed were to reconsider his behavior in terms of the company's goals rather than his own objectives as a sales manager, he would see prospecting as a means of increasing sales volume, rather than as a task that he should make John do because it is his job. Once prospecting was presented to John as a means of increasing his sales and therefore his commission, he would be more inclined to respond favorably to stepping up his efforts. Now, if the goals of both Ed and John are more in tune with each other, the results would increase the chances of meeting corporate objectives. (See the bottom half of Figure 19.)

In summary, there is no single, all-purpose, "best" style of management behavior that will maximize effectiveness at all times. Effectiveness is the result of a manager's modifying his or her own instinctive behavioral style to what is appropriate to meet the demands of the situation created by the behavior, attitude, values, goals, and maturity of the salesperson. The key to a manager's success lies in learning to diagnose that environment.

Management Style at Work

The manager's instinctive behavioral style may not be the best style for a particular situation, even though this is the style that the manager will be most comfortable with. Fortunately, we can learn to modify our instinctive style for the most effective one if we can understand the concepts involved and identify what that style should be.

Referring again to Figure 18, we will see that as the manager applies a different style to meet the varying degrees of maturity in the sales force or in an individual salesperson, certain relationships result. Furthermore, these relationships can serve as a positive or negative reinforcement to the situation, depending not on the intentions of the manager but on the perception of these intentions by the salesperson or the sales group. (See Table 1.) Now let's examine the various maturity levels to which the sales manager may have to respond.

Low Maturity Level in the Sales Force

Assuming a low level of maturity, response, or relationships in the salesperson or sales group, the effective style of the manager

Table 1. Effective and ineffective style relationships.

Maturity Level	Quadrant	Objective	Possible Negative Effect
Low	I	Strict control. Manager gives exact instructions to be followed.	Too restrictive. Resentment, with resultant mechanical following of orders.
Medium-Low	II	Partial control by salesmen as long as policy is followed.	Low-maturity salesmen will constantly question the manager's ability. Will see the manager as not sincere.
Medium-High	III	Manager willing to permit independent selling effort and direction.	Manager seen as "buying favor." Too loose for good direction.
High	IV	Complete control and direction by sales force.	Manager seen as more involved with outside interests. No leadership or direction.

would be represented by high-"D" behavior. The manager's objective is to tell the sales force what is expected, outline the procedures to be followed, and otherwise maintain strict control of the activities and output of the individual or the sales group as a whole.

But there is never a black-and-white, do-or-die relationship when it comes to interpersonal behavior. In the first place, neither the salesperson nor the manager is a pure temperament—that is, high-"D," high-"I." Instead, we are all a mixture of the four temperaments, each balancing or otherwise qualifying the others. Dr. Geier identifies over 1,300 combinations in his profile studies. What makes the theory work at all is, as we noted previously, that most people have one, or at most two, dominant temperaments dictating their behavioral reactions. Thus, as laymen, we can discuss any individual behavior, including our own, in terms of the "high" temperament. For example, I am a high "I," with a high-"D" secondary temperament strongly modifying the "I" component of my behavior.

In a like manner, a manager's behavior in response to any situation is neither totally right nor totally wrong. This also involves a continuum, with the result being more effectiveness or less effectiveness rather than right or wrong. Furthermore, while I have talked about applicable behavior for both the individual and/or the group, seldom will the maturity of the group be so uniform as to allow one style to predominate. Yet I can talk in terms of an overriding style because of this very factor of dealing with a continuum. Again, it becomes a matter of more or less effectiveness.

> Adam is the sales manager for a group of relatively new salespeople. While not all are new to selling, they are all at a low level of maturity in terms of company policy, procedures, product knowledge, and even their territories. The most effective behavior for Adam is to insist on strict and uniform following of detail in all of their reporting relationships to him. Each time he meets with them, he makes an effort to redefine their goals and reinforce his careful supervision.
>
> Sheila is another sales manager in a very similar situation. Instead of the strict control insisted upon by Adam, Sheila chooses a different style. Rather than issuing detailed instructions she prefers to discuss procedures openly with the sales force, allowing them the freedom to vary their approach to a certain extent as long as the overall objectives are met. Sheila's behavior is more representative of a high "I." Her behavior is certainly effective but, given the low maturity of the group, would probably be less effective than Adam's.

The above is not to imply that all new employees should be subjected to high-"D" behavior as the most effective approach. The manager must assess their maturity level, which is what determines the appropriate behavior for that particular sales group.

> Sheila noticed that several members of the sales group were not responding to the freedom her style allowed. She quickly changed to a more directed high-"D" behavior when dealing with these individuals.

Medium-Low Maturity

As the experience, and hence the maturity, of the sales force increases (or should increase), the more effective managerial behavior style will be that found in quadrant II—lessening the task emphasis and being more responsive to the people relationships that are developing. Sheila's behavior, described above, would be more effective in this instance than would Adam's.

Just as there are degrees of effectiveness emanating from the behavior style the manager employs, given the maturity of the group, there are also degrees of ineffectiveness if the wrong style is chosen or used.

Misjudged Maturity

If, for example, the actual maturity of both Adam's and Sheila's salespeople was greater than either had assumed, both their styles would have been ineffective. As more often happens, if the level of maturity and experience of both sales groups was perceived by the groups themselves to be higher than it actually was, the same ineffectiveness would be the result. In either case, Adam's group would feel too restricted. As a result, they might find ways to circumvent his authority, or they might follow instructions to the letter regardless of the outcome. Sheila's salespeople would see her as not knowing how to take charge, although they would certainly feel slightly more comfortable with Sheila than with Adam.

How do you handle the salesperson who perceives his or her experience and maturity to be greater than they actually are? The key for the sales manager is to understand both the actual level of this maturity and the perceived level. Managers must modify their own styles to meet the actual level, certainly being aware of the misperception on the part of the sales force or the salesperson.

> Mike thought of himself as a mature, professional salesman. He had been selling for various firms in related fields for eight years and had been with his current firm a little over two years. Although he had not met his quota in either of those years, he sincerely felt it was not his fault, instead blaming poor market conditions and product service problems for the lackluster result. Mike's last manager had not spent much time with him in the field, which Mike was comfortable with, since he did not feel he needed the close supervision. As a new sales manager, Steve immediately traveled extensively with each salesperson in the district and recognized that Mike was not the professional he thought himself to be. As Steve reported to his own superior, "Mike has had one year's experience eight times, not eight years' experience."

Steve could present a high-"D," quadrant-I behavior pattern, which Mike would surely resent unless it were softened by Steve's understanding both of Mike's needs and of Mike's own perception of his maturity in the job. As we will see in a moment, Mike needs a reason to accept Steve's effort at controlled direction—he needs to change his attitude. On the other hand, Steve could present Mike with a higher-maturity behavior. For example, he could bow to Mike's perceived "I don't need your help" maturity as indicating a high level of professionalism and respond with high-"S" behavior. The result would mean comfort for Mike, but no improvement in effectiveness. Thus, Steve has no choice but to approach Mike with a management style based on the actual level of Mike's maturity— and let the chips fall where they may.

> Steve pointed out to Mike how he could have been missing past sales through his own misunderstanding of the sales situations he had faced, and they discussed different sales strategies that could have been employed. Using the "gap" theory as a starting point to assess the needs of the territory, Steve and Mike agreed to several short-term objectives that Steve felt would help Mike identify new business. Steve also pointed out the need he had for certain call-report details that Mike had been failing to supply, "to let me know what is going on in your territory." It appeared to Steve, as he continued to maintain his control, that Mike was sincerely trying to comply. Steve felt that as Mike achieved successes in following his direction, his attitude would become even more positive. Should Mike fail to respond, Steve would have no choice but to recommend termination.

Medium-High Maturity; High Maturity

As the maturity of the group or individual progresses, a more effective style would be the manager's willingness to allow independent decisions to be made by the salespeople in all aspects of territory management. When the group has reached a level of professionalism, the most appropriate managerial style becomes one of "consultant" and "policy explainer" rather than "boss." Again, the danger in assuming a higher maturity level than actually exists lies in letting the sales force feel they are not being given any direction, even though this may not be the case. The "looseness" of control, properly applied, becomes an illusion—a perceived freedom from restraint—while the knowledgeable manager always remains ready to pull it back.

In actuality, effective management behavior is an ever changing, ever modifying and adapting cycle. The group as a whole may require a professional approach, while one individual may need stricter control, even in just a single area. A salesperson may be given complete freedom in developing sales strategy and tactics for a key account and yet need strict rules regarding travel expenses or call-report timeliness.

Style Flexibility

We have discussed effective managerial behavior as being something a knowing manager can turn on and off at will, being primarily dependent on the understanding of a particular situation. Unfortunately, this ability to be adaptable seldom comes that easily.

> Stan, a new sales manager, is 28 years old. Basically, Stan has a high-"S" behavior pattern. This temperament was formed through the first 18 to 22 years of his life, and while he continues to experience and grow, those 28 years of being an instinctive high-"S" reactor are pretty well entrenched. Certainly, Stan can adapt his behavior to meet the assumed needs of his salespeople, but under pressure—and time is a pressure—Stan will readily fall back on the pattern that he is most comfortable with: the high "S."

Fortunately, perhaps, for most of us, flexibility in style is not the only requirement for management success. In addition, our own salespeople will instinctively exhibit a good deal of flexibility of their own in meeting whatever style of management behavior they are faced with in terms of the mood of their manager. On the other hand, we have been discussing the most effective way a manager can meet a series of varying conditions. Thus, it is left up to the determination and professionalism of the manager to look for the best way to lead and not abdicate the helm to the sales force.

The difference between the inherent temperament or personality of managers and an effective managerial style is one of perception. The manager's personality includes his own self-perception, his goals, and the way he is. The managers' style includes how he thinks others see him, and how others actually see him in relation to the way the others see themselves. When sales leadership is ineffective, consciously or unconsciously, sales performance is as much affected as if sales ability were low. Management does make the difference.

8

Running a Sales Meeting: Why Not Just Call the Nearest Hotel?

"Hello, Boss! I got your message to call you."

"Glad I could catch you so quickly. I wanted to fill you in on our plans for a sales meeting for your area. We'll be leaving it up to you to make all the arrangements and run the meeting proper."

Well, there it is. It was going to happen sooner or later, because being a meeting planner is one of the jobs of being a sales manager. It sounds so simple a task. Yet how many times have you sat through meetings and watched one thing after another go wrong? Not necessarily big things that will break up the meeting, but all the little items that, added together, make a meeting run smoothly, make everyone comfortable, and make your boss say sincerely, "Darn good job!"

More than a "how-to," this chapter is also going to be a "what-not-to" discussion—a look at all of the fine points that go into making a meeting, training session, or conference run smoothly. Assuming that you or someone else has planned the content of the program and established the method by which it will be presented, we will examine the mechanics of staging the meeting itself.

156

Now, let's consider the planning details necessary to ensure that the meeting runs smoothly. For purposes of discussion, we will group these details under three main headings:

Physical arrangements
Personal-comfort considerations
Material-presentation details

Physical Arrangements

The facilities utilized for various types of meetings can range from bare essentials to the elaborate. The key factor, as always, is the matter of budget. Because of this, it is almost impossible to compile a list of physical factors that would apply to all meetings. However, we can present a list of arrangements and necessities that should at least be considered for any meeting and then examine some of your alternatives.

Seating Arrangements for Large-Group Discussion

Past experience has proved that the most favorable seating arrangement for a group discussion is around a round table. Each member of the group can see the faces of the other members involved in the discussion. Thus, we begin with a consideration of the most effective arrangement. Unfortunately, the round-table arrangement has three serious limitations:

- Maximum capacity is controlled by the size of the table, which in most instances is limited to 10 or 12 for comfort considerations.
- A tabletop stand to hold a presenter's notes, if required, becomes a barrier very quickly. It is a clumsy arrangement.
- If a presenter is going to use a flip chart or easel and pad, too many participants will be forced to turn away from the table to see properly.

When such problems present themselves, the answer lies in modifying the concept of the round table: A large square can be formed by butting rectangular tables at the ends or by using the same arrangement in an open U, letting the presenter stand in the open portion. This arrangement has all of the advantages of face-to-face communication and none of the basic drawbacks.

What limits there are to the open U are primarily a function of room shape. Keep in mind that what you are attempting to achieve through the seating arrangement is twofold: face-to-face communication between the participants to as great a degree as possible and as close a proximity between participants and presenter as possible.

As a rule of thumb, the open U reaches practical limits at 30 to 40 participants. Assuming tables seating 4 on a side, this would establish limits of from 12-12-12 to 12-8-12 for the number of participants who could be seated along each side and the back of the U. Thus, a narrower room would limit such an arrangement by putting the back table too far proportionally from the presenter, and a wider arrangement would put the members seated on each side too far from each other. Remember, we established such an arrangement on the basis of the need for mutual discussion during the meeting. Thus, mutual discussion by the entire group is going to be practically limited to the foregoing arrangements for reasons of proximity alone.

Seating Arrangements for Presentation

Interestingly, the open U, as described above, is also an excellent arrangement for group presentations or training meetings where most of the audience is focused on a presenter or "front" of a room. Equal to the U in effectiveness is the so-called schoolroom arrangement in one of its many versions (see Figure 20). (As you look at Figure 20, consider which of the seating arrangements shown would best meet your requirements if you were conducting a training program for 20 of your salespeople.)

What little difference there is between all of the schoolroom setups lies primarily in the size of the room and the number of participants. Practically speaking, the "standard" and "open-V" arrangements (including the double- or triple-row "open V") are limited only by the size of the room. In a formal-presentation type of meeting, the seating arrangements will be of less importance to communication than such factors as acoustics and type of visual display equipment, which we will discuss below.

Figure 20. Variations in schoolroom arrangements. Which would
work best for your training program?

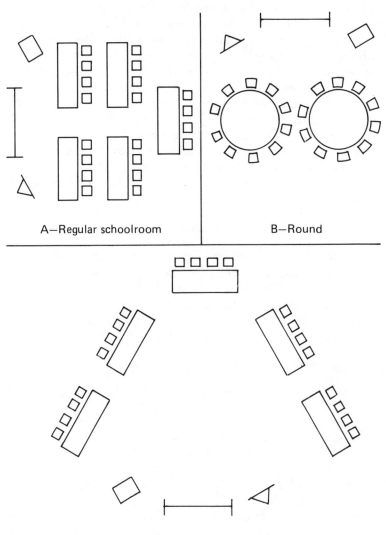

A—Regular schoolroom   B—Round

C—Open V

Most hotels and meeting places can supply narrow tables (approximately two feet by six or eight feet) which can provide adequate writing space for almost any size meeting. However, you should insist on a room large enough to hold full-size tables wherever possible, particularly if any considerable amount of writing will be done or a workbook is to be used. This is simply a matter of comfort and convenience for the participants, just as not squeezing chairs too close together can facilitate the spreading out of materials. If a hotel or meeting planner will not or cannot comply, find another meeting place.

However, using larger tables does present some practical limitations on the number of participants. Experience dictates that such limits, although difficult to pin down exactly, would be between 40 and 60 participants, assuming that they sit 4 to a table and face forward.

Some Other Seating Arrangements

Consider a training program where the participants will be asked to conduct further discussion in small groups. Here a series of tables holding 8 or 12 would normally be called for, particularly if their group discussion will be an important part of the program. Some variation of the arrangement shown in Figure 21 could be used.

Meeting-Room Necessities

Also included in the meeting room should be all materials and facilities necessary to ensure that the audience is comfortable during the meeting, including:

- Chairs as comfortable as are available.
- Paper and pencils for taking notes.
- Ashtrays, if smoking will be permitted.
- Ice water and glasses.
- All the miscellaneous but useful items that add to the smooth functioning of a meeting, such as extra pens, pencils, markers, chalk, masking tape, pencil sharpener, hole punch, pointer, paper clips, stapler, calculator, and so on, and so forth. (Just take a box and go through the office. The safest rule is that if you decide you won't need it—you probably will.)

Figure 21. Schoolroom arrangement modified for discussion groups.

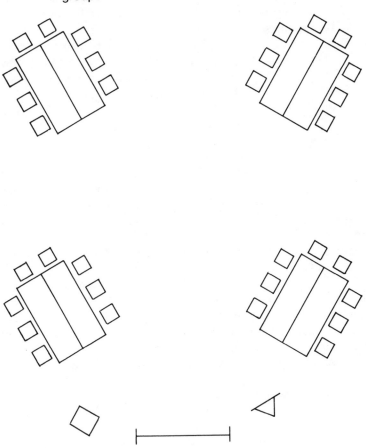

Personal-Comfort Considerations

Various factors must be considered to ensure the personal comfort of meeting participants. A pro or con decision regarding smoking has become a significant issue for meeting planners in recent years. More traditional personal-comfort issues include the adequacy of such factors as heating, lighting, temperature regulation, and control of distractions in the meeting room, together with arrangements for meals, breaks, and other refreshments. A final consideration in this regard is the mechanics of working effectively with the sales or catering staff at the meeting site to ensure that the personal-comfort arrangements you make for your participants are in fact carried out smoothly. Therefore in this section we will take a brief look at these and some other seemingly minor areas that can make a big difference in determining whether a meeting functions smoothly.

Smoking or Nonsmoking

It was not too long ago that the topic of smoking versus non-smoking didn't even come up for discussion. If you were setting up a meeting room, you made sure there were ashtrays. If someone chose to sit between two cigar smokers, he could complain, but not too loudly. Today, if you are going to do a good job as a meeting planner, you have to give some serious consideration to just what stand you will take on the subject.

Unless you are in California, there really are no set rules—unfortunately, not even those of simple courtesy. Know your own company is the first guideline. If you do not, ask. There is nothing more embarrassing than to announce to the entire assembly that smoking is prohibited during all sessions, only to have the president and four vice-presidents walk in and light up at the back of the room.

The following come under the heading of some approaches you might consider:

- Isolate smokers in one corner or at a separate table. (However, this is effective only when nonsmokers outnumber smokers at least four to one.)
- Announce smoke breaks each hour. Ban only cigars and pipes. Let smokers leave when they have the urge. (But none of these approaches will work satisfactorily, and all will be a negative factor in the meeting.)

Is there an answer, then? Yes. Unless you like crusades, find out what has happened in past meetings. If no one has really complained or made an issue of smoking, let it alone (that is, continue past policy). If your title is big enough and your peers and superiors will support you, go ahead and do what you want, but do not "play with the issue." State your rules at the outset and stick by them—at least until the next meeting.

Meeting-Room Comfort Factors

Lighting, temperature, and ventilation should be given careful consideration, so that your audience may do their best work during the meeting. If the meeting is to be held in the summertime, make sure the meeting room will be properly air-conditioned. There is nothing more deadly in any meeting than an overheated room, unless it be the overheated room where the air conditioner makes more racket than the speaker. Unfortunately, if you are not holding your meeting in a large, centrally controlled, fairly new meeting place, your odds of maintaining a tolerable temperature level over an eight-hour period are just not very good.

An effective meeting, in essence, is the sum total of group thinking. And most of us are unable to discuss and absorb problems thoughtfully in the presence of distracting influences—especially noise. Yet it seems that no matter how many assurances a hotel or meeting place gives, it invariably schedules a major renovation for the room next door to begin approximately one hour into your meeting or 5 minutes after you have introduced your boss or just after the president of the firm has made the opening remarks of his 40-minute talk.

There are two precautions you can take. The first is to double-check the assurances of no construction work. Also, have your hotel sales or catering manager check to see who will be in the next room. Having an auction going on at the same time can be worse than construction. The second precaution is to take some time and use some common sense in examining the meeting facilities with an eye toward potential distractions.

- Do kitchen doors open into the meeting room? Kitchen fights or trays of breaking cups are never carefully scheduled—except during meetings.
- Where will the coffee service come into the room? Ideally, coffee breaks should be held in the hall, but in a small meeting, this may not be feasible. Be forewarned, anyway, of a possible distraction.
- Visual distractions, too, must be considered. I recall one

meeting room that had sliding glass doors leading to the pool area. It was an ideal room in every way, except for the cute bikinis parading back and forth in front of the windows. I even lost my speaker.

- If at all possible, insist on luncheon's being served in a separate room. There is no way a hotel staff can set a lunch table behind a screen without causing a disturbance to your meeting.

If you cannot have it your way, go somewhere else. It's your meeting, not the hotel's.

Coffee, Tea, and Food

The meeting you have been asked to pull together will last two days. Salespeople and headquarters staff will arrive at various times between early and late the previous evening. The meeting is scheduled to kick off early the next morning and run the full day. The second day should wind up about 3:30 P.M., and everyone will head home. How would you handle the breaks and meals?

If you take the easy way out, you will leave everyone on his own the first evening, except that you will personally meet your boss and his entourage at the airport and have dinner with them (which, if it is in the hotel dining room, will be interrupted three times by arriving sales groups, and which, by dessert, will have expanded from the original 5 or 6 to a table for 15, all eating in different stages; those who are not there went barhopping, which will be very evident throughout the following morning).

The next day, you will schedule breaks at 10:00 A.M., with coffee and rolls, and again at 2:30, adding soft drinks to the coffee and those now-stale rolls left from the morning break. Lunch (fortunately held next door in a separate room) will consist of juice or fruit cup, then roast beef or creamed chicken, mashed potatoes, and peas, ending with either ice cream or pie. Those who did the town the night before will loudly insist on their right to several drinks and will be supported by the national sales manager, who secretly wants one himself. Need I continue?

This scenario, as I said, does represent the easy way out, simply because that is the way most meetings are handled. Hotels are used to the routine, and there is safety in running with what the crowd expects.

Now I am certainly not being overly critical. I have run too many meetings that way myself. But for those who would like to add just a bit of flair to their meeting, here are some suggestions.

Arriving the Night Before.   Since all participants are going to eat (and drink) anyway the evening of their arrival, why not use the momentum of the occasion in a positive way? With a two-day meeting you will probably plan a full dinner for the evening after the participants get in, so here are some alternative ideas for evening-of-arrival arrangements:

- Have a buffet and open bar. Depending on the numbers, you can have it set up in a meeting room or a suite, which could double as a bedroom for you or some of the junior staff. (Never put your boss in one of these unless he or she likes to keep going half the night.)
- Arrange for an informal buffet or pool party.
- If you enjoy entertaining, consider hosting a get-together at your house.

Breaking Up the Meeting Day.   There is nothing wrong with a big breakfast, but think about getting things going with coffee, tea, juice, fruit (optional), and rolls in the meeting room half an hour before the meeting's scheduled start. You can announce it the night before or leave a note in everyone's hotel box upon arrival. (Incidentally, I recommend that "leaving a welcome note" touch. It can be as elaborate a newsletter as you wish, but essentially, it brings everyone together at the opening gun with a minimum of confusion.)

Arrange for coffee refills at midmorning and again in the afternoon (there are always coffee drinkers at meetings). For the afternoon break, try fruit juice and/or fruit and yogurt. (Don't overdo this. They served us yogurt twice a day for three days at one meeting. Now I've got another suggestion for what they can do with yogurt!)

The second day, try the same routine in the morning, or plan a full buffet breakfast for variety. When the meeting will close at 3:00 P.M., you do not need an afternoon break.

Lunch. The word is "eat light." Try soup and a sandwich or salad. The second day, you might increase the calories, since participants can sleep on the plane, and most will be eating light going home (airline food is nonfattening, since there is never enough of it). Do arrange for participants to be able to order a drink. No hotel should have any problem in having a waiter or waitress on hand when participants enter the luncheon room. If they will remember anything from the meeting, it will be this gesture on your part.

Dinner. I have little to add at this point. The major consideration will be budget, but that has to be taken into account with everything. I would suggest planning to hold this meal at a different location, if only for variety, and I would also suggest a private room if at all possible. Naturally, transportation logistics will have to be factored in, and you might be better off choosing a hotel for the meeting on the basis of its ability to present a variety of meal options.

Working with the Sales or Catering Department

All right. You are ready to select your meeting location, so you are going to have to talk to the sales and/or catering department of a hotel or meeting place. All such staffers are going to try to be helpful—remember, they are salespeople with a specific product. Thus, you have to start by knowing what you are looking for and be ready to shop around to find it. Just as in every buyer/seller relationship, prepare your list of what you must have, what you would want to have if the price is not too high, and what you are willing to give up as a trade-off for a must or a want.

You can save yourself some time and hardship by proceeding in a series of steps:

- *Step 1.* Make a list of as many hotels, meeting centers, and resorts as you can think of in the area in which you want to hold the meeting. Arrange this list in your order of preference.
- *Step 2.* Start with the bare basics: how many will attend, how many sleeping rooms (single or double), and the arrival and departure dates. Now start with your list from step 1 and find out which sites will have adequate space to handle the meeting. (Remember, you will want separate dining fa-

cilities if at all possible.) My suggestion is that you proceed down your list until you have identified at least two or three locations that might possibly fit your requirements. When you have become familiar with the various meeting setups in your area, you can zero in on your favorites.

- *Step 3.* Visit each potential meeting site you have selected that has available space. If the sales people are doing their job, they are going to try to close you. Expect it. But you are the buyer. Tell them quite honestly that you have another location to check out but will contact them as soon as you can. If you lose the space to someone else, don't worry about it. There are plenty of places to look, and you know what you want.

Here are some points to keep in mind when dealing with the meeting place you finally do select:

- Work with only one person in the hotel meeting center, or resort. The individual's title is less important than the enthusiasm with which he appears willing to serve your needs.
- Do not leave messages for your meeting contact with anyone else in the facility. You cannot assume he will get them.
- If you are having materials shipped to the meeting, make sure they are marked to the attention of your meeting contact. Then let your contact know what to expect. I had one meeting almost ruined because materials shipped to my attention by my headquarters were refused by the hotel receiving department, since its staff did not know who I was. At that point, all the "We're sorrys" in the world will not help.
- *Do not assume anything.* Even though you have made and confirmed all arrangements, review everything and reconfirm just prior to the meeting date.

Material-Presentation Details

When you plan the presentation of material during the meeting, you should consider (1) the use of audiovisual equipment and (2) the mechanics of presenting material by other visual means. Under the audiovisual category we will discuss such items as slides, projectors, and various types of microphones. In addition to audio-visual equipment, the meeting planner must be familiar with the use of easel pads, blackboards, and overhead transparencies. Our discussion will include some do's and dont's for writing on a visual aid during a presentation as well as how to word the entries written on the visual.

Audiovisual Equipment

Some years ago, a news item appeared in *Advertising Age* magazine headlined, "Split Atoms? Sure! Run Slides? No!"

Anyone who has been subjected to presentations from any standpoint—either speaking, running the show, or just watching—has got to be aware that at some least foreseen moment, something is going to go wrong. That fact has not, as far as I can see, stopped anyone from making maximum use of audiovisual equipment whenever available.

However, while we cannot control the inevitable, we can take certain precautions that will limit the embarrassment to a surprising extent. The following list is based on my own experiences, not only as a speaker and seminar leader but as an active member of the National Speaker's Association. Hence, I have been able to include the combined expertise of the nation's best. In essence, their advice is summed up in two rules:

Don't assume anything!
Do check everything!

Showing slides? Even though you just checked every one before leaving home, run through them again before the meeting—all the way through. There is always the one that got in upside down. Check both the controls and the length of the extension cord for the advance controls. (I almost pulled a carousel projector off its stand once when I assumed I had an extra length of control cable just because I had specifically asked for it!)

Check the focus before the meeting; it saves fussing with it during the opening of the talk. Check the angle at which you will be projecting. Viewing is often more comfortable if the screen rather than the speaker is at an angle to the audience. This will depend heavily, of course, on the room arrangement and audience size, but it is something you should most certainly take into consideration when setting up.

Just because someone else is bringing his slides, do not assume your responsibility ends with making sure the equipment is in the room. It is still your show, and the speaker will be eternally grateful for your thoroughness.

Finally, take a moment to make certain there is a spare bulb. Equipment-rental firms are exceptionally good about supplying spares, but there is always the possibility of a slipup. If you find a spare missing, get on the phone. Bulbs always burn out when you think you can get by.

Using video equipment—motion pictures, overhead projectors, and so on? Every caution covered in the foregoing commentary applies. Check everything. Know where the fuse box is. There may not be much you can do, but it will certainly look as if you are in control until the maintenance people arrive. (Incidentally, commit hotel emergency numbers to memory, or at least carry a list of them around with you.)

Keep calm, whatever you do, and remember the adage, "The show must go on!" If your speaker has any presence of mind (few staff people do, it seems), he can find some way to keep things going while someone takes care of reviving lifeless equipment. If the speaker has done any amount of speaking, it will have happened to him before.

> Not long ago, I watched while Dr. Charles Dygert from Ohio State University made a presentation at a National Speaker's Association workshop. Dr. Dygert had just put a transparency on the overhead projector, had turned to the screen with a dramatic gesture to indicate his point, and . . . no picture! He never missed a beat. "Right there!" he snapped, indicating the blank screen, then moved smoothly to an easel pad standing to one side of him and kept right on with his point—to the warm applause of his audience.

Incidentally, always have an easel pad and stand handy—even if no speaker has requested one. People always find they can make a point better with a piece of paper to scratch on. (The pad and stand should be provided even if those in the back cannot read the message. They're an emergency tool!)

Using a tabletop or free-standing microphone? Get there early and check it out for tone and sound level. Ask someone to sit in different parts of the room while you are "testing: one, two, three." This also gives you a chance to discover where the controls are and how they function.

Using a lavalier microphone? In addition to the tone and sound level, carefully check the neck cord. These have a habit of being tied too short or too long and coming with a broken clip. Frankly, I would feel embarrassed to have my boss struggling to get it on while the sales force sit and grin.

> I neglected to check the cord on a lavalier mike the third day of a meeting. It had been all right for two days. Unfortunately, the last speaker the day before had been a little rough and left the clip broken. Now I always check every morning, and if I am the speaker, I check again before my own presentation—but that comes under the category of rechecking everything.

Visuals and Their Use

One of the objectives of a meeting is to stimulate the thinking of audience members. If the meeting is for training, an additional objective is to develop the reasoning power of the various group members. Such thinking and reasoning are encouraged by the use of properly framed and presented material. Some kinds of materials are more often than others of such a nature that they require visual display. When do you use one type over another?

When the divisional or headquarters staff is bringing the show to you, you do not have much choice in this area. Someone has already made a decision on materials, and your responsibility is to make sure the proper equipment is on hand, set up, and working properly. But suppose you do have a choice?

To make this section meaningful to the average field sales manager, I have to make some assumptions—the first of which is that, at some point in the meeting, you will have the responsibility of preparing materials for somebody's presentation, possibly your own. Second, I am assuming that your meeting will be limited in size, as will your budget. Thus, your choice of visual aids comes down to how to most effectively use an easel pad, blackboard, and overhead transparency.

Easel Pads and Blackboards.   In a word, always include easel pads. They are readily available, are reasonable to have on hand, and add a touch of professionalism to any meeting, even when they are not used. Just check to make sure there are workable markers on hand and plenty of clean paper on the pads.

Blackboards, in contrast, are awkward, dirty, obsolete—and still around. Why do we continue to use them when easel pads enable you to create a semipermanent record so easily (tape a used sheet to a wall or elsewhere in the meeting room) or get rid of what is not wanted (flip a page over)? If you need more room, you can use two or three pads side by side. If you do use a blackboard, make certain that adequate chalk and erasers are available.

Charts and Their Use.   The first stage of charting is to select the essential data to be brought out and emphasized during a meeting and enter them on an easel pad or overhead transparency. Such material can either be prepared beforehand or developed during the meeting. You can readily purchase transparency materials in any office supply store. Transparency materials can be hand-lettered by crayon if more elaborate charts are not required.

Writing During the Presentation.   When the speaker turns and writes on the pad or transparency, there is a tendency for discussion to stop. This is not necessarily desirable and tends to slow down the meeting pace. In addition, it requires effort and time on the part of the leader to start the discussion again. To avoid this situation, the speaker should carefully study the group and decide how best to maintain discussion while writing. Some of the more common methods used by conference leaders include having the leader talk while writing on the pad or transparency by

Reading out loud.
Expanding with additional remarks on what is being written.
Asking for a case to illustrate what he is writing.
Addressing some new question to the group.
Asking for additional items or thoughts to be added to what is being written.

The leader can also encourage the group to talk before writing by asking, "Now, what are some of the other items in this area that should be considered?" And when a response is started, he can turn to the board or pad and write the preceding item while the new thought is being stated or discussed.

My personal feeling is that I would prefer to work with a pre-completed set of charts for the sake of continuity and clarity, unless what is being charted is the result of spontaneous discussion. I have often worked with two pads—one preprinted and the second blank for notations during the meeting.

Wording the Chart Entries. The most important rule to remember about the wording of any chart entry is to capture the idea or thought expressed. Do not make your chart work a word-haggling session with the audience. Use your own judgment and make changes only when necessary to clarify a point.

What types of material should be charted? Generally speaking, consider charting all of the information that can be classified in any one or more of the following categories:

1. Information that will stimulate the thinking of the group or help them analyze a problem.
2. Information that will crystallize group thinking.
3. Information that must be referred to during the meeting to prevent misunderstanding or duplication of thought.
4. Information that must be referred to continually or would need to be noted again as the meeting progresses.
5. Information that will keep the meeting on target or help the group to think logically.

To Summarize: A Checklist for Your Meeting

BASIC DATA:
  Meeting dates and times.
  Advance meeting schedule, if possible (to plan breaks, meals, and so on).
  Number attending (include VIPs by name).
  Sleeping rooms (single or double).
  Equipment required.

PREMEETING CHECKLIST:
 Confirm registration list for sleeping rooms.
 Coffee breaks (each day).
 Meals:
  Confirm location.
  Finalize menu.
  Select beverage and/or bar setup.
  Make any necessary special arrangements.
 Meeting room:
  Confirm numbers and arrangement.
  Finalize time schedules.
  Confirm special arrangements or equipment.
 Audiovisual equipment list:
  Schedule or use of equipment during the meeting.
  Microphone, if required, and type of mike.
  Equipment table, if needed.
 Miscellaneous:
  Lectern (tabletop or free-standing).
  Extra tables or chairs.
  Special room arrangements.
  Easel pads or blackboard.
  Welcome notes or packets for participants.
  Handout materials, materials being sent.

ON THE DAY OF THE FUNCTION:
 Before dinner:
  Contact catering manager or maître d' to confirm arrangements and numbers expected.
 At least 30 minutes before the meeting starts, check:
  Microphone operation.
  Audiovisual equipment operation.
  Meeting-room arrangements.
  Availability of all materials (make a note of missing items; do not trust your memory).
  Shutoff for telephone in meeting room or arrangements for calls to be handled by the switchboard.
  Markers, chalk, erasers, pencils, and so on.
  Coffee or other refreshments if ordered prior to the meeting (check with catering to reconfirm schedule—*don't assume*).

Lighting controls properly set.
Ice water, glasses, ashtrays as required.

And finally, check on the whereabouts of the speaker or staff.

We were starting our meeting at 1 P.M. right after lunch. By 12:50, no speaker was in sight (nor had he been heard from since early the evening before). I found him in the hotel bar. He might not have worked directly for me, but it was still my meeting.

9

Training the Sales Force: What Makes an Effective Sales Program?

Restaurants are wonderful places to observe the world around you. Just the other week I sat close to a company affair that was obviously part of a sales training program. The group had apparently been meeting all day and had been joined that evening by the sales manager, who spent most of the evening telling them how to sell—his way.

"How'd the role playing go today?"

"That was fun. . . ."

" . . . I don't know what you really get from such sessions. Why, I remember my selling days. You get in front of tough buyers and you just picture them without any clothes on. Puts them in their place. . . . Then I remember the SOB we had to take out on the town to get an order. . . ."

And one hour later: "I think it's good we have opportunities like this to get together and share ideas. It's the real way to learn."

As a manager, your success depends on the people reporting to you—and those people, as salesmen, are not born fully developed for the job of selling, any more than you were. No matter how thorough and competent their previous training and experience, every sales position is going to be different—if only because every company and every product are different. The very essence of being professional lies in continued learning. To do the job, every salesman you have is going to need some of the knowledge and skill that got you where you are. How they get that knowledge and skill is what we call training!

No one can train salesmen once a year at the annual sales meeting, although it continues to give some managers a warm feeling to think their salespeople are being given such opportunities. This is a deadly attitude. Either you believe in training, plan it carefully, and do it regularly, or training will exist in name only.

In this chapter, I want to address two major functions and challenges in the job of the field sales manager. The first is coaching, which consists of on-the-job training of the sales force to reinforce those skills that develop them into professionals. The second challenge lies in the manager's need to expand the results of his coaching effort through the use of formal training techniques to build the sales organization into the most effective operation possible—performing not at 51 percent, but at 120 percent.

Coaching on the Job

Sid Haverman, the regional manager for Standard Machine Company, is traveling with one of his salesmen, Bob Fisher. Sid enjoys selling and actually welcomes these chances to get away from the administrative details of the office, but he wishes his salespeople would not rely on him so heavily as soon as a negotiation gets bogged down or a customer wants to negotiate a deal. Actually, each one of his salesmen is darn good in his own right, and Sid thinks they could actually get along very well without him. On the other hand, these accounts are important, and both Sid and his salesmen know they can't gamble with anything's going wrong.

They have just left the last of Bob's customers and are heading back to the office. "Old Mr. Grabow thinks he's a sharp negotiator," says Sid. "But you saw how I handled him. When you see him next week, don't let him get any more concessions out of you. He'll try. If it gets too tight, set up another meeting for me, and I'll get back into it. By the way, I liked the way you handled that product presentation with the engineering department. You really know your product inside and out."

Back at the office, Sid stopped by another salesman's desk.

"Joe, what's the update on that Harrington job?" he asked. The salesman replied, "Looking better all the time, Sid. We should be able to close it next month. I'd say we had a 90 percent chance unless Goliath comes in with a new twist. Then we may have to sharpen our pencils and negotiate a bit." Sid smiles, "That's great, Joe. Keep on top of it and let me know when you need my help to go back in."

Dan Brady is the regional manager for BWB Corporation. He has also been out on call, with Al Smith, one of his salesmen. It is near the end of the day, and they have just come from a customer. "Al," says Dan, "I think you called the shots with that last account, and your handling of Mr. Donnerman is just right for the type of personality you've pegged him to be. My hunch is you may be a little off in your timing, though. I think they are still looking at their alternatives. On your next call, see if you can get John Dobbs. He's on the finance committee, and he will be able to confirm whether they're budgeting for this and how much. By the way, I noticed you still tend to run sales points together in your presentations. Maybe you should slow down and let the customer do a little more of the talking. Use more questions between sales points." As they drove to the next call, Dan said, "As I recall, on this next account, you have been talking to the chief engineer about replacing the drives on his No. 3 line. Where does the sale stand?"

"Looks pretty good," replies Al. "We should close it next month." "Come on!" snaps Dan. "That doesn't tell me anything. Lay it out for me." Al smiles. "I'm sorry. I let that slip. I confirmed with purchasing that we are only 1 or 2 percent higher than Acme, but Ted Brooks in operations is really strong on our fast-time reactor feature, which he sees as saving him a lot of headaches in the future. I've been pushing him on that fact. Our objective today is to set a date with purchasing to discuss our offer." "Good," replies Dan, "I was about to ask you what action you wanted next. What's your game plan to get the negotiation meeting set up, and what part do you want me to play?"

In the foregoing examples, only one manager was using coaching techniques to train his salesmen. The other was still a "super-salesman." Yet the fundamental difference between the two managers boiled down to a language barrier. Both Sid and Dan were experienced salesmen. Both knew what had to be done. But only Dan understood and could express the concepts necessary to coach his salesmen in what should be done, so that he could feel free to let them develop their selling skills, while still knowing that in their shared understanding of the concepts, he and the salesmen could continue to communicate with each other. They could inform Dan of what was happening; he could guide them with his experience. Sid—instinctively knowing what should be done but unable to express his understanding to his salespeople—found it easier to be the supersalesman.

Coaching, by definition, is instruction or advice directed toward specific, observed, job-related performance. The manager is called on to translate what he or she sees into reality through the language of selling—the language most readily presented during sessions in the more formal methods of what we know as sales training. To make this transition, the manager uses the concepts and principles of selling (the language) to relate what experience tells him the salesman needs to do.

The Language of Selling

Here are some guidelines to help you start a serious, ongoing training program by taking advantage of the day-to-day coaching situations you will meet in traveling with your salespeople.

Before you launch into such a training program, remember that a soundly designed program does not have to be expensive, nor does it have to be conducted in a formal setting following a prepared script. It is not the exclusive function of the training consultant, the platform professional, or the staff assistant from headquarters. It will involve time, energy, and preparation—but mostly time.

Sales training consultants and personnel development specialists agree that formal workshop objectives and on-the-job coaching objectives are not the separate functions they were thought to be in the past. In other words, the effective growth and development of your salespeople come from a planned, coordinated formal training program that functions in conjunction with the day-to-day field guidance of those same salespeople in order to reinforce the concepts being presented in the classroom.

As a sales training consultant, I took my experiences in selling and presented them in a simulated real-world environment. To do so, I needed to be able to present those experiences in the form of concepts, techniques, and principles. Terms and definitions were needed so that the workshop participants could readily transfer their classroom learning to the real-world situations as they faced them. The expression of these concepts thus formed the language of selling.

Such formal workshops—presented on a group basis whether by a sales manager, a staff training specialist, or an independent sales consultant—have one objective: to help the participants in the program think. To help this thinking process, as with the study of any formally presented subject, participants must understand a common language. Language aids communication. Here are three brief examples borrowed from such workshops.

Example No. 1: Developing a Sales Strategy. When we study the buying/selling process, we discover that it proceeds through a series of identifiable steps or stages, beginning with "recognize need" (step 1) and ending, some ten steps later, with "order placed." Furthermore, the salesman is selling something different (and not always his product) to close each step. Different things can go wrong at each step, and any effective selling strategy will be directed at where a particular sales effort stands in relation to the entire process—that is, what stage the sale is in.

The "language" that allows a salesman and his manager to think succinctly about what is happening in a specific sale is what enables them to discuss the concepts and principles applying to this buying/selling process. It consists of the identification of each step or stage as well as the pitfalls, the determination of strategy objectives, and a shared understanding of how these steps can be used as a basis for developing a strategy or counterstrategy.

Example No. 2: Competitive Selling. One method for dealing with an entrenched competitor involves a two-part strategy called (as expressed in terms of the language allowing us to identify it) "competitive selling techniques." First, the salesman prepares his strategy by examining the criteria by which a buyer would measure any product (not necessarily that of the salesman) and then selling that buyer on accepting those criteria. The second part of the strategy lies in developing techniques for selling the product against the now-accepted criteria, not against the entrenched competitive product.

Example No. 3: The Psychology of Selling.   Selling is easy; people are complex. But people are what selling is all about. Referring to the concepts of behavior and knowing what they mean gives the salesman an understanding of the differences in buyers and how those different buyers will react to different sales approaches. It gives the salesmen a behavioral language in which they can communicate buyer behavior to the sales manager to enable them to develop a common strategy based on specific buyer needs.

Putting It All Together

Assume, for a moment, that both a sales manager and his salesman have been introduced to each of the foregoing concepts, through either a formal classroom exercise or informal reading and discussion. Here, then, is an example of what a coaching session might sound like. Let's listen in on a further conversation between sales manager Dan Brady and one of his salesmen, Al Jones.

Dan Brady and Al Jones have just left the offices of Richmond Corporation and are sitting in Al's car in the customer parking lot. (Parking lots are a familiar location for coaching sessions between salesman and manager. The location, however, should be incidental to the process, which could just as well have taken place later in Dan's office or somewhere else, perhaps over lunch. My point is that coaching is, or should be, an ongoing process.)

"Tell me, Al, how do you assess that meeting we just had?"

"Well, for one thing, it is pretty evident I thought the sale was in an earlier stage than it really is. I thought when they asked for a quotation on my last visit that it was only their way of asking for possible solutions to their production problem. Now I can see that they have fairly well made up their minds what they want and that the quotation request was really based on the sale's reaching a much later stage. As I told you when we went in, I thought we'd be able to get them thinking about an alternative offer."

"And now?"

"And now it's pretty evident they were just giving us the courtesy of meeting with them—that they accepted our bid as final and had already evaluated things, and not to our advantage."

"Where do you think you missed the right signs?"

"To be honest, I misread Bill Hayes, the chief buyer. I took it from his previous behavior that he wanted all those details and drawings because they were seriously looking for a better way to approach the down-time problems our competitor has been having."

"What kind of a personality were you working with?"

"Well, I thought from the way he reacted to my last visit that he was pretty dominant—'just tell me how to go at it' type of guy,"

"What we'd call a high-'D' temperament. Now what do you think?"

"You saw the way he reacted all during our meeting—particularly when the engineering group was in the room. If that's not a high-'C' personality, I'm still misreading something."

"I think you're right. That's exactly the way I read him. That's why I took the tactic I did back there."

"Yeah, I caught that. I'm glad you did."

"How does this affect your strategy now?"

"I've really got to face having General Acme in there pretty solid in spite of their past problems."

"Do you think you can come up with enough firm criteria to meet a competitive selling situation?"

"I think so. When we get back to the office, I'll put it on paper. Then could you give me your reactions? I also think if we can get our product people to meet with their engineers, we can still move the negotiation stage back to an earlier point, where we could be in a stronger position and have a better chance of success."

The foregoing was, of course, very sketchy, but it entailed Dan's and Al's using those three sales concepts outlined earlier. Building a common language for communication is one goal of coaching or on-the-job training.

A Philosophy of Coaching

We have looked at just one aspect of coaching—that which reinforces the concepts presented in formal training. What are some other uses of coaching? Let's begin to answer this question by considering the diverse functions of sales management. These would include (not necessarily in any order of importance):

1. Supervising the day-to-day activities of the sales force in terms of deportment, schedule, punctuality, and completeness of reports and assigned programs.
2. Collecting economic, competitive, and market data and feeding them to affected personnel.
3. Forecasting expenses and sales data.

4. Maintaining operations in terms of budgeted expense, supplies, and office administration.
5. Hiring personnel as required and approved.
6. Evaluating personnel effectiveness in terms of individual sales targets.
7. Directing activities of the sales force to meet quotas.
8. Training and developing the sales force for maximum effectiveness.

We can put all these activities of the sales manager into three categories: first, administrative functions (items 1, 4, and 5); second, marketing functions (items 2 and 3); and third, personnel functions (items 6, 7, and 8). Coaching is a technique for performing the personnel function.

To effectively meet the requirements of the personnel function, you have to know how your salespeople operate in the most critical aspect of their job—their face-to-face interpersonal relationships with their customers. One way to evaluate this is by asking questions and listening to how they respond. We call this counseling, and we discussed this in Chapter 5 in terms of the appraisal interview. A second way is through direct observation followed by feedback. We call this coaching.

We can break coaching down further. As a sales manager, I essentially want to be aware of how my salespeople handle any aspect of their job that could detract from their total effectiveness. Thus, I am there to observe any of the areas listed below—and then some. Here are both the areas and some ideas for getting into them.

Planning:
"Before we go in, what's your objective on this call? What do you specifically want to achieve?"
"I noticed you took a rather out-of-the-way route getting here. How could you have combined calls to cut down on your traveling?"
"When do you write up your call report? I always used to have trouble remembering if I waited too long to do them."
"What happened to your sample case?"

Attitude:
"I have the feeling you didn't care for that assistant buyer. Your feelings were pretty evident."

"Have you ever thought of showing up here early with rolls for their coffee?"

Knowledge:
"The benefits he was asking about were pretty clearly covered in our last sales bulletin. How well do you keep up with these releases?"
"How could you have explained these policy changes more effectively?"

Selling skill:
"Let's talk about timing when you ask for the order."
"Who else in a key buying position are you familiar with at this account?"
"Why were you so quick to give in on that FOB point?"
"Were you aware of having cut that engineer off in the middle of his explanation?"

Other items:
"You missed two good opportunities to probe while you were going through your briefcase looking for those price sheets. Have you thought about reorganizing your books?"
"What happened to the fender of the car?"

The basic rules of coaching are relatively simple:

•All comments are based on observation. As with most of the above areas, professional growth comes from a number of little things that can be improved before they become serious. Impact is always more positive when you discuss something that has just happened. Thus, the technique of the "parking-lot counseling" session has a prominent place in effective coaching.

•Regardless of the positive and helpful results to come, you are still criticizing. That is why each of the areas I mentioned above put the lead-in to the discussion either in the form of a question ("Why did this happen?") or in the form of self-criticism ("I've had this problem also").

•KISS (keep it simple, stupid). Do not overload the salesman with a long list of what he has done wrong. Pick one, or possibly two, of the more critical items and turn the discussion into a real learning situation with these. You will find, human nature being what it is, that if the salesman has a weakness in a minor area, it will tend to repeat itself, and you can bring it up later or during a counseling review session. ("I've been noticing something I think you're probably completely unaware of doing.")

•Under no circumstances that I can think of should a salesman have to revise his call schedule because you are going to spend the day with him in the territory. (I am not referring to those occasions when you want to visit a key customer and so inform him of a change in plan.) Yet plan it as you will, salespeople do rearrange things so you will see them at their best. Perhaps it is a matter of survival, but your objective is to help them grow, and you can do this best in their natural habitat. (I have even gone to the extent of first asking for a detailed list of planned calls, then telling them I am going to go with them. That seems to work once with most, and twice with those who are a little slower.)

As is so true with most interpersonal relationships, I cannot give you an effective script to follow beyond what has already been said. What you will regard as important will be a product of your own successful selling. What you choose to say and how you choose to say it will be a result of your individual management style. The final result should be the development of an increasingly effective sales force.

Let's Tie Coaching to a More Formal Program

All companies are in constant need of aggressive, creative, and resourceful salespeople to get their products accepted and used by customers. Without informed and capable field sales representatives, a company cannot hope to compete. But how many have ever stopped to consider the fact that good salespeople—the kind who can help a company grow—do not just happen? There is no such thing as a "born" sales rep, because selling ability is more than an instinctive feeling for what to do. It may start with that, but it goes much further.

Selling does require certain native abilities, which are contributing factors to success. But these are obviously not the only factors. If salesmen don't know their product or their customers, if they cannot apply what they know, or if they do have a positive attitude toward their product, their company, their customers, and themselves but have difficulty making things happen or determining what action to take, they need to be trained.

This brings us to an important crossroad as far as training is concerned, because there are two schools of thought as to the best means of accomplishing this:

- Some feel that experience alone is all that is necessary. They argue that every time a salesman enters a selling situation he learns, and given a number of these experiences, he will soon learn all he needs to know.
- Others feel that sales training can best be accomplished by combining experience with a planned and a continuing formal program.

Granted that experience is an important factor in the learning process, but experience alone cannot be relied on as the best teacher for two reasons: First, experience alone is costly. While a salesman is gaining the necessary experience, many sales are lost. Further, gaining experience is a lengthy process—so lengthy, usually, that the salesman remains nonproductive for too long a time. The second argument against relying solely on experience is that experience alone is ineffective. In the long run, the salesperson learns in "bits and pieces" and only in those areas with which he or she has contact on a regular basis. Further, experience gives sales management no established means of checking on the salesman's progress. Thus, erroneous and unhealthy skills and attitudes can develop to a danger point, resulting in a loss of efficient and effective selling. The best means of development, then, is not experience alone, but experience in combination with a planned program.

To capitalize on the necessary personal traits, good salesmanship demands training in three areas:

Knowledge of products, customers, and customer organization and environment.

Skill in the application of this knowledge to the interpersonal aspects of selling.

Development of a favorable *attitude* on the part of the salesman as it affects his approach to his knowledge and applied skill.

Let's see why these three areas are so important.

Knowledge continues to increase in importance owing to three factors:

- The narrowing differences between competitive products. As objective differences between products become more difficult to distinguish, buyers rely more and more on emotional factors in making their purchasing decisions.
- The higher rate of introduction of new products, which increases the need to inform salespeople of the changes.
- The speed of the advancement of the art. Buyers are becoming extremely knowledgeable and professional.

> For a number of years, I have taught an evening class on production and inventory control at a local college. As a result of adding to my own knowledge, I was able to "talk shop" with a major customer, thereby gaining greater respect from him for knowing something of the problems he was facing.

More and more, the salesman is called on to become more than a "pitchman" to his customers. Pressed for solutions, customers look to the salesman who can understand what is going on in their industry, not merely take orders.

Skill is needed for effective communication. Attitude brings the selling effort to life.

Determining Training Needs

Some training is needed for all salespeople. Even the accomplished salesman who has been selling for many years needs training on new products and a continuing review of his selling skills. As a rule, it is always better to overestimate rather than underestimate the amount of training required.

The task of structuring a requisite, relevant, realistic, feasible development program can be carried out according to the following formula:

The requirements of good salesmanship
minus
Those requirements your salespeople already meet
leave

The total development needs of your people,
of which
Those needs common to the majority make up
your group's development-program content
and
Those needs common to one or a few make up
the individual development program
to be handled through coaching or counseling.

The following is an exercise you can use as a sales manager in determining the training needs of your sales force. This can be developed in conjunction with other managers, as a group exercise with your salespeople, or as an individual project.

Step 1: List all of the *areas of competency* required by the sales force. In effect, what are the things your salespeople do to make them good, to make them successful in their job? For example:

1. Identify potential users.
2. Determine what step the sale is in and your position in relation to the competition.
3. Identify the customer's needs and level of awareness of those needs.
4. Develop a sales strategy with specific actions for key sales negotiations.
5. Etcetera, etcetera, etcetera. . . .

Of course, these areas would vary according to industry, type of selling, and type of customer called on. This completed list would cover all the critical areas your salespeople should be proficient in.

Step 2: What would be a *standard of competency* for each of these areas? When you observe your salespeople in the performance of each of the areas of competence, what standard would you measure this performance against?

Step 3: Along with setting a standard for each competency area, how is attainment of the standard to be measured? What *basis and method of evaluation* will you apply to each standard? (Table 2 shows a useful way to format the information gathered in steps 1, 2, and 3.)

Step 4: What are the current capabilities of your sales force?

Table 2. An example of the assessment of training needs: competency areas, standards, and evaluation bases.

Competency Area	Standard	As measured by
1. Identify Users	Be involved in 60 percent of ongoing sales negotiations.	Ratio of quotations to number of customers.
2. Determine stage	Identify by guideposts.	An 80 percent level of accuracy in reporting status.
3. Identify needs	Actively promote need development.	Meeting 75 percent of specs.
4. Develop strategy	Present sales tactics on sales over $450,000.	Closing 80 percent of negotiations.
5. Etcetera	Etcetera	Etcetera

How do your salesmen stack up, as a group or individually, against these competency areas, as measured by the standards established for each area?

Step 5: What does your sales force, individually and as a group, need in order to bring them from their current level of capability (step 4) to a level where they will meet the standard for competency (steps 2 and 3) in each area established (step 1), as categorized by each of the following:

- The *skills* required
- The *knowledge* necessary
- The *work habits* or *attitudes* needed

When you have completed an exercise such as the foregoing, you will have identified the training needs of the sales force—as a group and individually.

Where Do You Get the Programs?

Once you have decided on the needs of your sales force, you face the problem of where the program will come from to meet these needs. Unfortunately, the problem is compounded by the huge variety of program content and presentation choice that does exist.

But to simplify matters let's separate all programs into three categories: those designed and presented by outside consultants, those generic purchased programs designed to be presented by the sales manager, and those programs you put together and present yourself. They all have good and bad features, but the first measure is cost—how much you can spend!

The Professional Consultant.   Regardless of whether you go all the way and bring in a sales training consultant or whether you just purchase a generic program that you yourself will present, you are faced with a major caveat: "How do I get what I think I'm paying for?" "Training consultants" can be found in abundance through the Yellow Pages, booking agents, local and national directories of the National Speaker's Association, a host of corporate training managers, and respective industry associations. Their fees run from several hundred dollars to over $3,000 per day (and in a few cases even higher), usually plus expenses. Some include all materials, and some charge extra.

Unfortunately, you cannot even use price as a guide. Whatever the price charged, some few are excellent; a great number are very good; some just starting out could be good but need more seasoning; and as in any industry, some are not worth the effort no matter how low their price. More to the point, cost may not relate directly to quality in your specific case. Obviously, somebody thinks such consultants are good or they would not be able to command those high fees. But what they are presenting—their own selling experiences, their current client list—may not fit with the training objectives you are looking to fill. When you do find one who fits what you need, you will probably also find he is worth the fee. Such consultants are professionals—this is how they make their living.

If you are going to hire a sales training consultant to carry all or a portion of your program, it is vital that you begin by knowing exactly what you are going to want to achieve. Do not hesitate to tell your consultant what those objectives are. If you want to turn a green sales force into a group of professionals in a two-hour program, the consultant should be the first to tell you to save your money. You may buy a lot of entertainment value, but you are not going to get much lasting behavior change from a two-hour keynote speech.

Many years ago, when I was just beginning to find my wings as a fledgeling speaker, I was asked to keynote a sales meeting for an industrial paint company. This was the firm's annual meeting, and it was the specific wish of the president that I give his sales force a short, 2½-hour presentation on the need for increased professionalism in selling. This, I was told, was the highlight of their two-day work-sun-golf-drinking program. I would close the meeting right after an "awards luncheon" on the second day.

Unfortunately, the president chose to finish off his awards speech with a 20-minute harangue of the sales force, during which he threatened to fire half of them, increased their quotas, cut their expenses, and changed the commission schedule. Oral Roberts himself wouldn't have had a chance after that.

In short, a consultant can bring a tremendous amount of professional selling technique to your training program, but he cannot perform a miracle. Be certain you know exactly what it is you are hiring the consultant to accomplish.

Do not hesitate to check out any and all references. Ask for sample materials and an explanation of the consultant's methods. I do not know of any qualified consultant who cannot or will not openly supply references, materials for examination, and even an audiotape or videotape for a demonstration of his style.

Buying a Generic Program. As with so many things—know what you want to achieve when buying a generic program. Ask for references and sample materials before buying. *Generic* programs are exactly what the word means: They have been generalized for use by a wide variety of industries, salespeople, and companies. Most of the cost is in publishing the materials—thus, the need to sell to diverse groups. What you are buying is preprogrammed materials to which you will have to add the language and specific situations appropriate to your company and sales force. What such programs do is give you a guide to follow as the presenter. Your program will be as effective as you are in making the transition from their generally presented concepts to the specific.

Generic programs primarily tend to cover the more basic sales concepts. If this is what your salespeople need, such programs can save you a good amount of time in preparation. But you have to make the program yours in order to make it work!

Building Your Own Program. Let's suppose, for whatever reason, you want to "do your own thing." Where do you start? Once again, you must first know what you are trying to achieve. If it is knowledge, there is probably more than enough in the combined experiences of your sales group. Your job will primarily be that of leading the group discussion, of keeping the discussion on target, and of starting it off and closing with a summation. If one or another of the group has certain relevant experience, you might make him a part of the discussion by specific request, allowing him time to prepare beforehand.

If you feel you need to reach into the area of selling skills, you must develop a language of those skill concepts you will present. The best place to begin is at a library or bookstore. Use concepts pertaining to areas of selling you want to cover to outline your presentation. After an opening introduction, use your skill as a discussion leader and let the sales group develop their own dialog. Be prepared to introduce additional key thoughts from your reading research and bring in such skill-practice techniques as role playing between various members to enhance the discussion and bring home specific concepts you feel the group needs training in.

What Makes a Good Sales Training Program?

A good sales training program is never a hit-or-miss proposition. There are fundamental principles that help people learn. After all, training is not something you do to or for someone. Learning is a phenomenon that takes place within the person and is a direct result of the person's effort to learn. Training is merely the intentional act of providing the means through which that learning can take place. Experience may be a good teacher, but you cannot count on it when you have specific skills to teach in a limited time period. Let's examine some of the rules of learning that should be kept in mind as you prepare your training program.

Motivation to Learn. Salespeople must be motivated to learn, just like all adults. Never assume that anyone will accept a training program just because it exists. Bear in mind that you are training mature adults who are often college graduates. People today are more sophisticated than they used to be. In fact, most salespeople want a training program that they can "sink their teeth into." Whatever you do, do not present material that tends to "talk down to them."

Frequency, Recency, Intensity.   Once people are properly motivated, certain other factors enter the picture in determining the amount that they will learn. The human brain is composed of some 10 billion neurons, each with numerous "feelers" or "extension wires." When we think, remember, or imagine, these neurons discharge an electrical current, thereby creating a path or groove that, once made, tends to recur. The probability of recurrence depends on the frequency, recency, and intensity of the stimulus.

The more often any connection is made, the stronger it becomes. The pathway over which the nerve current travels becomes more deeply worn. Remember this when you next try to get a new idea or item of information across to the sales force during either group or individual training. The old-timers put it this way: "You tell them what you're going to tell them; you tell them; then you tell them what you told them." Do not assume that a single explanation of a point will stick. Find ways to repeat important points—in different ways at different times to avoid boredom.

Making the Presentation.   Three basic methods of training are telling, skill practice, and group participation. Your use of these methods is determined by whether your training program primarily involves the imparting of knowledge or skill.

The least effective training techniques are reading and telling—particularly telling by lecture. Studies show that we remember only about 10 percent of what we hear, and any sales manager who has tried to get a written message across has already discovered, to his frustration, how little we recall of what we read. Fortunately, there are several aids to reading and telling that can make them more effective.

If you are training in a "knowledge" area, the use of visual aids will help. The prepared easel pad and overhead transparency can be economical aids, as we discussed in the preceding chapter.

If you are training in a "skill" area, on the other hand, the skill has to be experienced to be learned. Skill practice involves the whole person. People not only hear and talk about situations; if skill practice is properly done, they experience them emotionally. This is the instructional value of such an economical technique as role playing. Properly handled, there is probably no more effective skill-training tool available.

But perhaps the best training technique of all is the guided discussion, since it also develops attitude changes. In this method, the leader, who already knows where the discussion is heading (perhaps from having purchased a generic program), asks the group a series of questions and eventually guides the group to a set of conclusions.

Skilled discussion leaders will go out of their way not to express their own opinions. Rather, they direct their effort to drawing ideas from the members of the group. They avoid posing as an authority or "answer man" and instead permit the group to reach their own conclusions based on discussion of their experiences.

Following Up.   To be effective, every formal training session must be followed up. If too much time has elapsed between learning and doing, little change will take place. This is a basic argument against the "once a year" training session at the national sales meeting. Training sessions should be followed up by review sessions at specific intervals or on-the-job coaching, using the formal concepts as background.

> Last fall I was asked to design and present a four-day selling-skills program for an industrial sales group. Some six months later, the national sales manager asked, "Do you think the sales force are using the skills they were exposed to, or was it all a waste of time?" The answer, not surprisingly, was what you would expect. Where the regional sales manager, either because of his past experience or because of training as a trainer, reinforced the concepts covered, those salespeople were applying what was learned. In those regions where the sales manager did not reinforce the concepts and techniques covered, there was little evidence of continued application by the sales force.

Three individuals become involved with every training effort: the trainer (whether an independent consultant or the sales manager), the sales manager, and the salesperson. The success or failure, and the responsibility for performance, while interrelated, are different for each.

Individual	*The individual is responsible only for . . .*	*The training fails because of . . .*
Trainer	Presenting the material.	Poor presentation. Poor communication of material. Poor or inappropriate concepts or techniques.
Sales manager	Seeing salespeople develop and grow. Outlining training needs.	Abdication of training to the trainer. Lack of reinforcement.
Salesperson	Meeting sales objectives.	Inability or unwillingness to learn.

Now there is only one further thing for you to do with regard to training: *Start!*

10

Why Salespeople Fail:
Can I Do Anything?

Why write about sales failure in a book on sales management? For one thing, because selling is a business of failure, and because when the salesman fails, the sales manager fails. Perhaps, too, the topic must be brought up because by having a better understanding of why salesmen fail, the manager can do a better job of helping them not to fail.

The heart of the matter is that failure comes from many places. We have, indeed, touched on quite a few of them already. Failure is a concomitant of each chapter in this book, since failure is not an absolute measure, but often little more than a loss of effectiveness.

Thus, success or failure is often directly related to the understanding, the actions, and the professionalism of the manager. We neglect to establish and monitor needed objectives. We do not hire properly. We miss the opportunity to keep things going. We fail the sales force through the ineffectiveness of our own style. We do not train properly or for the area needed. We do not motivate. The salesman fails, but this is often just as much the sales manager's fault as the salesman's.

I began my own career selling industrial apparatus in Cincinnati for Westinghouse. It was not a glamorous, star-studded beginning. As a matter of record, those first days were downright miserable. I am sure I made every mistake there was. I certainly felt like it.

I do, however, recall being in the office of one of my assigned accounts late one day, and a plaque he had on his desk caught my eye. It was a simple statement by the philosopher Clausen, which said:

> Opportunity is a haughty goddess who wastes no time on those who are not prepared.

And it changed my life.

That plaque, even in its simplicity, awakened something inside me. Here I was, selling the products of a major corporation, in one of the major industrial centers of the country, and I was ready to throw in the towel because success wasn't falling in my lap. But I had a choice. I could go out there and win—or fail. And I would have to do it all by myself. Whether I won or lost was going to be on my shoulders, no one else's. I could get all the help I needed, but the ultimate result was up to me.

That evening I sat at the kitchen table and followed the advice on the plaque: I made some plans for my career, for my selling, and for my life. And among the goals I set was to learn everything I could about this business of selling—of dealing with people.

In the years to follow, I did become a good salesman, in the sense that I achieved my sales targets. Yet the road to professionalism remains, even today, quite rocky—and always uphill.

When the Skills Fail

I attended all the sales rallies. I sat at the feet of some of the best sales trainers in the nation as they stood before me on the speaker's platform and gave me their wisdom.

I remember listening to a speaker tell me how important the art of asking questions was to success in selling. He told me that the key to handling objections was to be able to turn the objection into a question. He said, for example, "Your customer says, 'Your price is too high,' so you reply, 'My price is too high?' And having changed that objection into a question, you have the buyer defending his statement." I tried that! The next time a buyer presented a price objection, I asked, "My price is too high?" and the buyer snapped, "You heard me!"

Another of the platform greats suggested that when faced with a price objection, one should draw oneself to one's full height, look the buyer right in the eye, and say, "I would rather defend my price once than my quality forever!" I tried that! And the buyer said, "Yeah, and I can still buy it cheaper from your competition."

I read all the books. I went to all the sales schools. I learned to probe; to determine need; to take all the facts and features about my product, turn them into benefits, and present those features and benefits to my buyer in sound sales points. I learned to negotiate, to develop a strategy for meeting an entrenched competitor; I learned to close.

Then I would go back out into the field and put all those things I had learned into practice, and as most of us have found, sometimes those techniques we had been taught worked, and sometimes they did not. Sometimes I won, but more often I lost.

A Selling Attitude

It was years later, when I was a manager of sales training, that an incident brought home to me what may have been happening. I gave a talk to a sales group on the techniques of time management. Their manager had complained, "They spend too much time in the office sitting around just talking." Well, we had an excellent discussion at that meeting. The salespeople joined in enthusiastically and contributed a number of good suggestions. Yet when I was finished, every one of them went back to the office and sat there for the rest of the day talking things over. And it occurred to me later, as I flew back to Pittsburgh, that the knowledge and skills of time management had little to do with people's effectiveness in the use of time—that it was each individual's attitude toward time and the use of time that made the difference.

I began to look closely at all the various aspects of selling—all the areas of knowledge and skill that everyone was saying were so important to selling success—and I found the same relationship holding in each. The key ingredient for success was in the attitude of the salesman toward the product, toward the customer, and yes, toward the knowledge and skills of selling.

The Words Used

We are sold things every day by the power of words to describe and excite. Corporations are spending hundreds of thousands of dollars to research words and to promote products, from toothpaste to air travel, by the power of the words used to present them.

Think of how important words are to your career. If, as a salesman, I asked your customers to describe you as they saw you, what words would they use? If today I asked one of your salesmen, or your superior, "What kind of a manager is he or she?" what words would they use to tell me? If I asked you to think of the very best salesperson you know and describe that salesperson with a single word, what would that word be? If I asked you to think of the most ineffective, the poorest, salesperson in your experience and to describe that salesperson in one word, what would that word be?

Interestingly, we have done just that in our sales seminars and have found, over and over, that some 85 percent of the words used to describe the best, and the worst, salespeople have been words that depict attitude. We asked people for a one-word description of a person who did a job either very well or very badly. But, rather than reflecting the person's level of knowledge or skill, as you might expect, the words most often chosen described *attitude*.

When I failed as a salesman, there were times when it was not the techniques and skills that failed; rather, the failure was in my own attitude toward those techniques and how I used them. As managers, we are called on to continually monitor the attitude with which the sales force meets its daily challenge. Perhaps, by understanding the importance of attitude to our salesmen's success, we can find the means to help them ride the roller coaster of emotion that is often inherent in the job of selling.

When Training Fails

When we train, we take parts of a situation out of context, study the concepts of the sales technique involved, and leave it up to the ability of the sales force to accept the training in those concepts and apply those pure concepts effectively in the real world. No wonder the techniques learned in the sales schools did not always work the way they were supposed to. We were applying them in the wrong situations or with the wrong timing. The answer, it seems, would be to develop training programs that are more in tune with reality, and not teach concepts out of context.

Thus, as manager of sales training, I turned to the use of the candid camera. We subsequently shot over 400,000 feet of film, candidly catching buyers and salesmen from a variety of industries in the real world of selling—and as a training device, we could not use any of it!

The problem was that there was too much going on in the real world to be able to effectively say, "Watch that salesman! See how he handles this!" Because in looking at the real world portrayed on our film, too many things were happening at any one time. Thus, to train, we must simplify action so that we can deal with the concepts and principles of a single technique and then leave it to the salesman to apply those concepts properly when the time comes to use them. Salesmen may indeed be failing from a misapplication of skills and techniques, but the sales training workshops are not finding adequate methods of helping them.

Is this a failure of training or a failure of the salesmen to grasp what is happening and apply the correct solution? We know today that a big part of the solution is for the sales manager to supplement that formal classroom training with on-the-job coaching. Thus, we now know that a share of such failure must also lie with the sales manager.

The 5 Percent Competitive Solution

Today, as before, the sales world continues to be a competitive battlefield where there are only winners. Few come in second and survive. We continually hear salesmen and sales managers complain that it is getting extremely difficult to sell successfully in today's highly competitive marketplace.

That certainly sounds like a reason for failure, but I tend to question its validity. Instead, any salesperson who wants to put in a little extra effort can move forward, not infinitesimally, but all the way to the very top of the list. What I am saying is that there is not as much competition out there as most think. If you can find a means to motivate your sales force just a little, any failure to meet your objectives should not be caused by tough competition. The reason is that less than 5 percent of the salespeople out there are really selling!

"Those are pretty strong words," you say. "Do you have some facts to back that up?"

Yes. I have a study: if you accept 400,000 feet of candid camera film—shot of randomly selected salesmen, from randomly selected companies, from randomly selected industries—as a valid study. Then I want to tell you, on the basis of that 400,000 feet of film, that less than 5 percent of the competition out there is selling. They are visiting, servicing accounts, making calls—but they are not selling!

What is the definition of selling? Selling means taking an action that induces another to react favorably to your firm in a way that has profitable results for that firm—a reaction that the other person would not have shown without the influence of your inducing action. That's being a salesman. If salesmen fail, it is probably not because of intense competition.

Selling Is Service

Our customers are reacting to us all the time. Regardless of whether we are conscious or unconscious of our actions, this reaction is taking place, and it is going to be positive or negative or passive without our control unless we are willing to do something about it. What is the problem? Salesmen have forgotten what service to a customer means!

As I noted in a previous chapter, buyers rely more and more on subjective emotional factors in making purchasing decisions because there are fewer objective differences between competitive products. I bring this point up again here since industrial sales managers seem to feel that all the emotions in purchasing are on the consumer side of selling.

The fact is that in all purchases, the product itself is coming to be recognized as the least significant factor in a purchasing decision, since the "product" is what the buyer perceives it to be. Accepting this, there are two important aspects of any purchase: the salesman as a personality and the service the buyer feels goes with the purchase.

As a salesman, I remember getting up at 2:00 A.M., driving 60 miles, and getting a warehouse manager out of bed to get me a bearing so I could deliver it to a customer whose line was down. How many salespeople would do that today? My study says less than 5 percent.

Not long ago I went to a major department store to buy a tape deck for my car. Two models were available. I asked the salesman what the difference between them was. He said, "I don't know. You have to read the instructions." No I don't! I later bought a unit from Radio Shack. (I take that back. I bought the unit from a young man working for Radio Shack who took the time to explain what I was buying and how to use it.)

I recently went to buy a pair of shoes. The salesman didn't even know how to measure my foot. If I have to fit my own shoes, I might as well buy from a catalog.

I don't buy my suits from a particular clothing store, but I do continue to buy from one particular salesman who caters to all my needs—who "services" my account.

The department stores have forgotten what service is all about. The management means well, but a salesperson keeps getting in the way.

In 1970, I was flying first-class on a major airline's dinner flight from Newark to Atlanta. The choice was steak or chicken. After half the cabin had been served, the steak was gone. I wrote to the airline's vice-president of marketing. He replied, "All our meal selections are by computer to determine the best selection and mix." I stopped flying on that airline.

Ten years later, a letter to the *Chicago Tribune* appeared in "Action Line" for Sunday, September 14, 1980. It was from a lady who, flying first-class on the same airline from Chicago to Miami, was offered a selection of steak or chicken, and they ran out of steak. In response, the manager of passenger service for the airline wrote that "Complimentary in-flight meals are planned using past history for both variety and ratio of selection—a vast majority of passengers are satisfied."

Built on a concept of service, the airlines of this country won handily over the railroads, which had forgotten what passenger service meant. Now it would appear the airlines, too, have forgotten.

On a recent trip, I stayed at a hotel that was physically better than average and had every appearance of living up to the highly advertised slogan of the president, committing the chain to "excellence in service." One almost insignificant human incident got in the way.

The "services" card in the room announced that breakfast would be served beginning at 6:00 A.M. At 6:10, the dining room was still locked. I went to the front desk: "What time does the dining room open?"

"At 6:30" (he didn't bother to look up, obviously having more important things to do).

"Your services card in the room says 6:00."

"We changed it."

"Why don't you change the card?"

"Because that's the way it is."

. . . at which point I didn't care if I ever stayed at another of that chain's hotels again. Such a small incident, yet in competition for today's buyer, that is often all it takes to lose both a sale and a future customer. The hotel industry is not a good example of what service means.

We are a part of the total environment we live in, and when the world around us forgets the meaning of service, what is to keep the industrial salesman tuned to the concept? Sloppy—or nonexistent—service is catching on and growing like a plague. Only the spirit of management can stop it.

Selling: A Business of Failure

In a very real sense, selling is a business of failure. Salespeople have to be willing to risk failure every day of their careers if they want to win. Just think, if a firm is striving to obtain 20 percent of a market, and a particular salesman has ten sales negotiations underway, he is going to lose eight of them making the objective.

When we look at the sports giants, we see them risking great odds, counting on their ability to win more than they lose. These heroes understand the risks of the game they are in.

The story is told of Babe Ruth, the great home-run king. It was a World Series, last of the ninth, two out, bases loaded, and New

York was behind by one run. The "Babe" came to bat; the crowd went wild with excitement; and . . . he went down one-two-three. In the locker room, a sports writer asked, "How does it feel to have lost the game?" Babe replied, "But I'm that much closer to my next home run!"

We look at the giants of the sports world, and we see them risking against great odds, winning and losing by large margins. But that is not what life is made of for most of us. As salespeople, as sales managers, even just as people living our day-to-day lives, winning or losing is more often a matter of little things, the small edge.

I had an aunt—Aunt Marion. Although blind from the time she was a little girl, she could tell the greatest children's stories anyone ever heard. As a matter of fact, kids used to come from blocks around to listen to her stories, and all the relatives used to urge her to put her stories in a book. Well, she was going to, but the state of Illinois and the federal government did her a great disservice. Because she was blind, she received free education, and the day she died, she was in the process of taking just one more journalism class before she started on her book.

Often, when salesmen fail, it is the little things that are at the root of it. It is so easy to be busy. Some of the hardest-working salesmen I know are failing, and they are working very hard at it.

The Buying Process as a Failure Factor

Often, failure to understand what is happening in a sales situation can cause a failure through poor timing or through selling the wrong thing. The buying process has been shown to consist of a series of identifiable steps or stages, which can demand varying strategies of the salesman. Studies indicate that selling the product itself plays an important role in less than 40 percent of that buying process. Yet product selling techniques continue to dominate sales training activities, and hence the salesman's effort. The great majority of salespeople today are identified solely with their product, and no salesman can succeed for long with just that to back him up.

In its essential elements, selling starts when the buyer (whatever his title: engineer, vice-president, purchasing agent) accepts the fact that a need exists—a need to do something different, to take an action. Now, at this point, the textbooks tell us that the buyer will seek a solution to that acknowledged need.

Don't we wish it were so! Unfortunately for a lot of salespeople, it's not. If you have been shoveling snow with a snow shovel all winter and your shovel breaks, do you start researching all the different ways of removing snow, or do you rush back to the same hardware store where you bought the last shovel and get another one? This, in turn, leaves all the salesmen of snowplows writing back to their home office that there is no market with you for their product—and besides, Ace Hardware has your business all locked up.

Right there is a failure point—the salesman fails to recognize what is going on. Sometimes all that should be sold is a solution to a problem, not a product the buyer does not even recognize as needed. Selling the product comes later.

When a buyer does determine a solution to his need, he establishes two criteria for every salesperson who will be selling the needed item. First, he establishes a set of constraints. These are usually physical and measurable. The buyer has so much time or space or money. Often, these are the factors we see as product specifications. At the same time, the buyer establishes a set of preferences or priorities. These are often more emotional than physical. They have to do with such factors as feelings and memories and perceptions. "I like you and your company." "I don't like your service department." "I like you but owe your competitor a favor." Salesmen may not like such things, but they have to deal with them, because more sales are lost in this area of priorities than in the area of constraints.

Every salesman has an obligation to understand the need, solution, constraint, and priority that are involved and, at every step, to know how he stands against the competition. Often, winning only involves having a 51 percent edge in these areas. However, if at any time a salesman finds that he does not satisfy a need, a solution, a constraint, or a priority, there are only two choices. He can change the need, the solution, the constraint, the priority—or he can change his product! And the easiest way of changing a product is to change the price.

Sometimes what is involved is not a failure of selling, but a failure to sell the correct thing at the correct time. It is the manager's role to continually question the sales force to determine how closely they are keeping tuned to each of their customers. Do they know what is happening? Do they have a sound sales strategy to control what is happening?

The Greatest Reason for Sales Failure

All of the foregoing brings us to a discussion of what is possibly the greatest single cause of a salesperson's failure. It lies in misunderstanding the very cornerstone to the sales process—the concept of establishing need.

Every salesperson has been told that nothing happens until the buyer has a need. Every salesperson accepts the fundamental truth of such a concept and the purpose of need-development techniques. There it often stops. I know of few authors who treat the subject in any detail. I know of few sales training programs that go beyond the skill of asking probing questions to get at a buyer's need level. As important as the concept is as a reason for failure, I do not know very many salespeople reporting a lost sale because "the buyer didn't need us."

With so much riding on need development to establish a successful opening to a sales effort, it is imperative that the sales manager fully understand all aspects of this concept to be able to effectively guide the sales force through the pitfalls inherent in building any strategy around need. Often, it falls to the sales manager to be objective enough to see where these pitfalls lie.

The Psychology of Need

Let's start by complicating what has been a simple concept up to now—a simple concept on the face of it, yet the truth is that need psychology is as complex as anything could possibly be. It should be, since it is wrapped up in the very nature of humanity— humans are indeed complex entities.

We tend to consider need as singular. Need is never singular. At any moment during our selling, that *buyer* (I use the term generically—he or she could carry any title, perform any function) is motivated by three needs: The buyer has an organizational need, because he is a part of a company, with its own unique set of objectives, goals, and needs, either openly expressed or simply a part of the culture of that firm. Second, the buyer is faced with the varying needs of the job. Being a purchasing agent, engineer, or whatever, the buyer has needs imposed on him by the nature of that job function. Thus, the engineer has different job needs than the purchasing agent. And finally, the buyer has personal needs, which he looks to satisfy in all dealings with the surrounding world, both the world within his own organization and the world outside the organization.

Just to add a further complication, the same three areas of need exist for every person involved in the buying process. The purchasing agent has organizational, job, and personal needs; his or her boss has organizational, job, and personal needs; and the engineer or manufacturing supervisor or whoever else is involved likewise has these three need areas to be considered. The salesperson, in turn, has his own set of needs, and if the sales manager gets involved, you add still another set of needs.

Selling Need

Furthermore, consider that a buyer will accept the need to change or accept a new idea or product under only three conditions—when he or she sees:

A different way of doing something.
A better way of doing something.
A danger of deterioration of the way he is currently doing something.

Thus, the salesman faced with selling the need for his product or service is faced with selling one thing—*dissatisfaction!* He is not selling a product; he is selling a reason for change, and that reason adds up to buyer dissatisfaction with things the way they are.

The Mental Process of Need Acceptance

Whenever a buyer is asked to accept a new idea or concept, or as in the case of the sales situation, the buyer is asked to buy a product or service, he mentally goes through a series of steps. Essentially, these mental steps begin with a perception or awareness that a need might possibly exist. Then a potential attitude change toward the need or toward the situation surrounding that need enters the process before there is even a final acceptance that the need does indeed exist. We are not done yet, because research also shows that the buyer will still go through a mental trial run, or provisional acceptance of the idea. That is, the buyer tries it on mentally, then goes through a further weighing or evaluation until finally arriving at the point of resolution and adoption. Only now has need been established.

In any sales situation, all of these steps may move rather rapidly, perhaps in the few minutes a buyer might give a salesman to present the product. On the other hand, it could be a rather drawn-out process, covering the span of several sales calls. The important point is that the buyer will not have accepted a need until after going through these mental gymnastics, and this can have some important meaning for any salesman who hopes to sell to him or her. Let's look individually at each step in this need-acceptance process.

As already noted, nothing of importance is going to happen in a buying situation until that buyer recognizes and accepts a need that grows out of dissatisfaction. The buyer must see a better way to do something, or a different method, or a danger of deterioration of a present method. Thus, one of the central tasks facing the salesman introducing a product into an organization is to create an awareness of the need for the solution that product represents—and that eventually means dissatisfaction with the present situation or with the current use of a competitive product.

This is where it all starts. Yet, as with so many selling concepts, it is much easier to state than it is to accomplish. Since we are dealing with a rather complex receiver called a human being, there are some built-in barriers that tend to complicate the process, right from the beginning and on through to final acceptance.

Three Barriers to Communication

Barrier No. 1 is "selective attention." This makes the buyer likely to hear some messages (to a greater or lesser degree) and ignore others. We all do this. We have a tendency to "tune out" what does not have meaning in light of our current feelings about what is happening in our world. It has to do with the way we listen.

As you may know, we all have somewhat different listening patterns, which tend to filter input and which might even differ from one day to another. If the buyer is not mentally tuned to the sales message, the sales effort will have a difficult time getting started.

The second barrier is "selective retention," which has a bearing on what we remember and what we conveniently forget. The buyer may hear the sales message, but higher-priority events come along, and that takes care of that. You can see that even the most brilliantly planned and executed sales presentation is already up against it right from the start.

One of the difficulties salespeople experience throughout their selling, but perhaps more predominantly in the early stages of need awareness, comes from a human tendency that psychologists refer to as "functional fixity"—so-called tunnel vision, which reduces the ability to see the broad picture, to see the forest rather than just the trees. This is the third barrier to communicating need awareness. Surprisingly, little was known until recently about "functional fixity." Both the role it plays in communication, particularly in need awareness, and how widespread it really is have been misunderstood. Let me give you a problem to solve by way of analogy.

Suppose I were to take you into a room that is bare except for two strings, each hanging down loosely from the ceiling. Your job is simply to tie both loose ends of the strings together. However, the distance between them is such that you cannot reach one string while holding onto the other. Now the only objects in the room to help you are a small book of paper matches, a box of birthday candles, and an electric disconnect switch.

To solve the problem, you tie the box of candles to the end of one string (the matchbook is too light and the disconnect too heavy) and start the string swinging back and forth while you grab the second string and neatly catch the swinging string in your other hand as it comes toward you.

Would it surprise you to be told that in a psychological study, it was found that only one in 37 adults could solve this problem? Or to learn that the reason most failed was that when they looked at the candles, all they could see was a decoration for a birthday cake?

I proposed this problem to an industrial purchasing agent, an executive with a major corporation. He sat there looking off into space for a minute and then said: "I can't see why you would want a disconnect switch. There's nothing electrical there."

This tells us something very important about selling—which is, after all, the art of getting ideas across to others. As the saying goes, "The myth of communication is the assumption that there is any!" Faced with such obstacles, the salesman again and again hears the familiar, "I'm too busy," "See me next time," "Our line is full," "Your price is too high!"

Even at this point, if need is triggered into awareness, it is now going to run up against some further resistance in the "attitude" of the buyer toward a lot of factors, including the salesperson, his or her company, the competition. Perhaps the buyer feels powerless to do anything about changing a spec or adding a new product in spite of his now-growing awareness of a need or dissatisfaction with the situation. Perhaps politically, the buyer just does not want to "fight the system" within his own organization.

Even with a "good" attitude, the buyer might feel that change is not appropriate at this time or that a superior might be against it—anything that could make the sales presentation less than a legitimate fit at this time. This tells us that even when a buyer sincerely accepts a need for change, the sales effort could be rejected because the timing is politically out of sync. It tells us that even if the sale reaches this point, it could lose out when the buyer mentally tries the idea on to see how it will fit with his organizational plans. In essence, the buyer makes a psychological purchase and weighs it for fit, or organizational comfort, including his own comfort with the idea being proposed.

We tend to talk about selling need as a single mental step, going from a condition of unrecognized need to one of need acceptance. We think of it as a single step: Need is not recognized, and then it is. Yet we have just covered five steps—perception, attitude, appropriateness, mental trial, and evaluation—and each step brings with it its own series of barriers or resistances to the selling effort. How can your salespeople fit this into their selling strategy?

The Techniques of Selling Need

Anytime an attempt is made to categorize strategy alternatives, there is the difficulty of presenting one or two methods and suggesting that these will fit most situations—either that, or being so general that the reader is given little help. On the other hand, working with salespeople from many different industries has shown me that there are several generic strategies that tend to be more effective at different stages. I can therefore present these with the understanding that the sales manager will be able to use them effectively as guidelines—as a starting point. The final strategy for a particular situation will come out of probing the specifics of that situation with the salesperson responsible.

Thus, strategies for the initial step—awareness that a need may exist—are best built on such concepts as "what the idea being presented does that others do not do or do not do as well" or "how easy the process is to understand." Such strategies are known as "relative advantage" and "complexity." But once you move to the "attitude" step, these "best" strategies may also change, and now you will find a better strategy to be "compatibility," or "how it will fit with a buyer's current thinking, use, or methods," or how "riskless" the change will be, both personally and technically.

Fortunately, you will also find that the "compatibility," or "how well it fits," strategy is also one of the better approaches in the "appropriateness" step, the third step. While in the trial and evaluation steps, some form of "how easy it would be to try it on a pilot basis" or "how easy it would be to discontinue without any adverse effect" would probably be best. Of course, during evaluation would be the time to bring in any cost or time saving inherent in the offer.

Perhaps the main point is that each step can mean using a different or varying strategy to achieve the most effective selling. More important, it means that the salesman must be aware that he may have to change his strategy to deal with these changing steps.

Up to this point, I have talked primarily of dealing with an individual buyer, but strategy considerations also have to take into account the organization behind the buyer. As you so well know, organizations vary in complexity—that is, in the number of departments or staff specialists who can get involved in a purchase decision. They also differ in formality, or the degree of emphasis a company puts on rules and procedures. And companies can differ in the degree to which buying authority is centralized or decentralized.

Thus, if you are going to consider developing a sales strategy to meet a buying situation where your salesman cannot seem to get started, you must not only consider where need awareness stands with each individual buying influence that is involved but you must also determine the nature of the customer's organizational structure. Is it primarily (1) complex (having numerous staff functions or departments involved in the buying decision), (2) formal (having rigidly followed rules or procedures for the introduction of a new product or idea), or (3) centralized or decentralized in its buying authority?

Developing Organizational Strategies. Shortly, we'll see how we might develop a strategy to meet each of these situations. But before we do, let's simplify things by dividing those six need-awareness steps into just two stages. We will call the first three steps the "beginning" stage. That covers perception or awareness, attitude formation, and appropriateness or fit. The latter steps—trial, evaluation, and adoption—we will call the "confirming" stage.

Hence, you have the "beginning" stage and the "confirming" stage. You can make this division because, although you are actually dealing with some six steps, when you begin to put together your strategy alternatives for each step, you will find that your strategies will tend to continue effectively across several of them. You thus find the continuing strategy to be merely an extension of your previous action. Also remember that although you will now be developing a broad strategy based on the organizational structure of the customer, each of the key buying influences in that organization must at the same time be approached as individuals—different and distinct personalities—and here the independent strategy elements for the six steps apply as we discussed before.

The following outlines the strategy base we will now discuss:

Type of Organizational Structure	Need-Awareness Stages	
	Beginning	Confirming
Complex	Facilitates	Hinders
Formal	Hinders	Facilitates
Centralized	Hinders	Facilitates

Research shows that, in general, where a firm has a highly complex organizational structure, this will aid, or facilitate, the "beginning" stage—the early stage. In other words, it appears that the many professional staff people who add to the complexity of an organization also add to that organization's readiness to accept new and better offers. Complexity of structure facilitates new and better offers. Complexity of structure facilitates the awareness factor, since the larger the group, the greater the odds that at least one or two individuals will be receptive to change.

On the other hand, that same organizational structure tends to hinder the latter, or confirming, stage. Remember, these are the trial, evaluation, and adoption steps. Apparently, it does so owing to the many more conflicting interest groups that compose that complexity and thus make it more difficult for the organization to come to any consensus or agreement on a proposed change. Thus, complexity aids the beginning stage and gets in the way during the confirming stage.

A highly formal organizational structure, in contrast, hinders the beginning stage—the awareness, attitude-formation, and fit steps. This appears to be caused by the procedural rules that are characteristic of a formal organization and tend to limit new information searches. Thus, such organizations are not very flexible when it comes to accepting alternative courses of action or changes in methods. However, such a structure, with its singleness of purpose, does appear to aid the confirming stage. That is, the highly formalized organization often has a clear set of procedures, which facilitate final acceptance of a need, if one does exist—just the opposite of the complex organization.

Likewise, the more centralized the organizational structure, the more the beginning stage of need acceptance is hindered. However, the hindrance in this case appears to happen because communication channels in a centralized operation, more often than not, do not provide information on the more negative aspects of situations, making dissatisfaction less apparent to those who might be in an authority position. And no need is established without dissatisfaction. However, a highly centralized structure aids the confirming stage, since a centralized structure, by its nature, offers a single buying authority, which can facilitate moving ahead once the need is apparent and is deemed to be appropriate.

If you are thinking this is all a bit complicated, remember all those orders your sales force failed to get off the ground because they could never get the need accepted.

Beginning-Stage Strategies. Now let's attempt to devise a sales strategy for each of these three organizational structures, starting with the beginning stage as we look at each.

Selling into a complex organizational structure, which favors the first stage, you would stress those unique advantages you offer that might make acceptance useful to more than one application or decision group. In other words, you would want to develop a strategy with multiple benefits for several influencing groups within the customer's organization. A possible alternative might be to find someone influential in that customer's organization who will carry the ball, particularly to move the sale through "attitude formation." Another alternative—again, particularly strong in meeting resistance at the "attitude formation" step—would be to show that a minimum of risk is involved in making any change.

With the highly formalized organization, which hinders the beginning stage, it becomes necessary to devise a strategy that can introduce awareness through whatever channels are established for information flow within that customer organization. Nearly every organization has a routine or procedure for the introduction of new ideas or for product changes. In selling, say, OEM components, this often begins with the project engineer or, if the components are for production equipment, with the plant engineer. The more formalized the organizational structure, the more specific and rigid the rules will be for such an introduction of change. It is particularly important that the strategy "work" with the formal organization. It is a matter of understanding the organization rather than an individual—of understanding how the organization wants to do business.

On the other hand, in the centralized organization, you often find there is a single individual who can be the key to initiating awareness. If you cannot find that individual or interest him or her directly, you may need to find a way to come at him from another angle—perhaps through an influential third party or a consultant. But that individual remains the key to your beginning-stage strategy.

Confirming-Stage Strategies.   Once awareness has been triggered, the use of a third-party champion to influence commitment is still a good strategy alternative as you move into the confirming stage with the complex structure, which tends to hinder by its complexity. Where the "champion" can be found, he can become an ally in leading your offer through the maze of organizational procedures to meet the mental trial and evaluation steps of the confirming stage.

Finding a champion is also a good strategy alternative in dealing with the rules and procedures that have been established by the formalized structure. Fortunately, with the formal or centralized structure, your salesperson's job is made easier in the latter stage of need acceptance because these organizational structures aid the confirming stage.

Once again, you have to understand how the customer wants to do business. As the confirming stage continues, you may need a strategy that assures the decision maker that he faces a minimum of risk in accepting your proposal.

With the highly complex organization, a strategy alternative might be to get a trial or pilot purchase by one group or another to prove your acceptability. Remember, the highly complex organization hinders the confirming stage, and you may have to go after confirmation or acceptance in smaller bites.

The Sales Manager as the Strategist.   It has certainly not been my intention to complicate what should be a rather straightforward concept. However, the absolute importance of developing need acceptance is so vital to any sales strategy that an in-depth understanding of the mental process involved is essential to the continuing sales success of any strategy dictated by the organizational structure your salespeople are selling into. Salesmen, even the best, are unfortunately more action-oriented than strategy-oriented. Experience tells us that when a targeted strategy is developed and put into operation, it is because the sales manager assumes the role of strategist, leading the sales force into the planning and pushing them for the results.

Besides using the material in this chapter to develop successful strategies, you are encouraged to use it as a group-discussion topic or in individual coaching sessions. Perhaps it seems too simple to suggest that the major attitudinal problems faced by the sales manager can be solved by systematically following such advice as is presented in the pages of this book. However, this is exactly the result intended to be achieved from following the managerial techniques covered in the foregoing chapters. All that remains is for the manager to apply these concepts, either to the sales group as a whole or to the individual needs of each salesperson. The material herein has shown you the way—now you still have to put it all together.

11

Putting It All Together

The sound from the headset attached to the arm of the seat came through undistorted: "United 705, you are cleared for immediate departure, runway two-six, wind two-eight knots south-southwest. Maintain vector to 8,000, contacting departure control on three-seven-seven-niner. Have a good day." "United 705—we're rolling." Instantly came that increased roar, while I was simultaneously being pushed back and down in my seat. The ground rapidly fell away beneath. We entered a realm of clouds billowing and full on all sides, until I felt I could, in the words of John Gillespie Magee, "put out my hand and touch the face of God."

"Good morning, ladies and gentlemen. This is your captain speaking. We're presently climbing toward our cruising altitude of 30,000 feet. The weather along our flight path will be clear and bright this morning, and we should arrive at our scheduled ETA. I'll be switching off the seat belt sign in a few moments, and the flight attendants will begin serving your breakfast. On behalf of the entire crew, we welcome you to the friendly skies."

I have never considered travel a hardship. Frankly, I find this a time for catching up—a time for reading, for making last-minute report changes or notations, or just for quiet contemplation. At one such moment, I chose this latter option, and looking down from my window at the miniaturized country slipping by beneath me, I could suddenly get a broader panoramic vision of all that has gone before us in the various thoughts captured within the chapters of this book. Now it was time to pull all the pieces together.

The View from 30,000 Feet!

The greatest difficulty throughout this effort has been having to write about single management concepts as if they could really be discussed by themselves, as if what we had discussed before, and would discuss again from a different viewpoint later, could stand in isolation—without any relationship to any of the other chapters. Once, a man who had been a lumberjack, a state trooper, a narcotics undercover agent, and a criminal investigator asked me what was in the mind of a business executive, successful when I knew him, who had later turned to crime. He was trying to understand him as a businessman. I didn't know how to tell him, because the investigator had never experienced the world of the manager. We could talk about specific instances, but we could not communicate regarding the total person—the business personality. We had to confine our discussion to the pieces. Well, we have also looked at all the pieces. Now it is time to put them together and see how they fit.

Every time you set out to hire a new salesperson, all that has gone before, everything that has already happened in that territory, has an effect on the person being hired. The "gap" discussed in Chapter 1 merely represents what is unknown in the territory. The concept is logical and basic. All I have done is express that unknown in a formula, an approach. Yet any manager should instinctively see that there is always a "gap" between what he knows, hopes, or thinks can happen and what he wants to happen—that the salesperson in that territory will make the quota, meet the objective. I believe the problem is that we, as managers, really do not think in terms of the "gap," the unknown, the "what has to happen," but concentrate instead on expanding the known. That does not always work.

Ed Smith sat staring at the booking records on the desk in front of him. The district was running at 80 percent of objective, and he did not see how he could meet his annual target in the time remaining. Acme Corporation probably wouldn't close until next year, and none of the others in the sales force were sufficiently ahead of quota to make up the difference. Ed began to think of all the reasons that justified the failure.

Certainly, Ed is not going to meet his target, not even with magic—not at this point. But Ed is also the victim of his own thinking. What is going through his head at this point is no more than the same concepts he has been living with all year. Sales success does not begin from "what we failed to do," but from "what needs to be done." Sales success this year started long ago—perhaps in the first quarter of the year, perhaps last year. Instead of thinking, "What didn't happen?" Ed should have been thinking, "What do I need to close that 'gap'?" That is the first step, and we started with it in Chapter 1 because there will be no success for the new sales manager until he catches on to thinking this way.

When Ed hires that new salesperson, his interview will revolve about the job specifications, the criteria of the job. Yet he must also hire someone who will fill the job with the very skills and attitude that were lacking in the previous incumbent.

Ed looked carefully at the sales candidate sitting at the table in front of him. He appeared to have all the qualifications for the job. Yet Ed felt a hesitation that kept nagging at him. The last salesman did not really cover the territory. In the last six months, he had been in one key area only twice—not enough to uncover the potential that should be there. Will this candidate be a "digger"? What is there in his background that will make up for what was previously missing?

Without being conscious of it, Ed is already using what we proposed in our "gap" approach to select his next salesperson. What we said in Chapter 1 made a start, yet it has already carried over into the selection process discussed in Chapter 2. Every people decision is a gamble. By basing it on what a candidate has to do, it at least becomes a logical gamble.

All a manager can measure is performance, and all that should be measured is performance. Personality, honesty, and all the rest do not measure anything; they are only part of the package. Performance is what ties everything in this book together.

A recent news item announced that some of America's basic industries were becoming more sophisticated in their sales approach. The gist of the article was that certain key manufacturers had "discovered" that the magic road to success could lie in determining through strategic planning what the customer wanted. They had discovered "that once a supplier gets the specifications written, it is too late to do anything but react"—which often means cutting the price (something sales managers and sales trainers have been saying for the past 30 years).

The question is, how do your salespeople do anything but react unless you, as a manager, have set the type of objectives that zero in on the specific shortcomings of their individual territories? The solution is not in a more sophisticated sales approach, but in a more sophisticated management approach.

> Cynthia Davis thought of the visit she had just completed at her major customer. The buyer, long a personal friend, had said, "Cynthia, there's not much we can do about this one. Engineering changed the whole design approach, and it looks like we won't continue to assemble the same way we did." Cynthia knew what she had to do. If her price were low enough, they might have to reconsider staying with the same components.
>
> Bill Robinson left his customer feeling very good. His work with the design people had kept him on top of their thinking. Building on this, his factory had helped him develop several alternatives that could be used to show the design people how they could save money by changing their design approach.

In one case, the salesman failed, and in the latter, the salesman succeeded. But suppose, in the first case, the sales manager had said the following to Cynthia Davis:

> "What makes you feel the situation here won't change?"
> "Nothing, really. But purchasing keeps me informed."
> "When was the last time you discussed future designs with engineering?"
> "Not recently."
> "Let's set this objective: By the end of the month, you will have discussed future design plans with the engineering department at each of your current accounts."

Maybe the potential changes would still have been missed, but I do not think that is an excuse for the sales manager's not taking the first step.

In Chapter 3, we discussed the process and the rationale for setting objectives against which the sales force could act. Chapter 4 took those objectives and expanded them so the manager could exercise control over the results. The point is that there is no way that we can separate the contents of those two chapters. Objectives are useless without a means of measuring their success or failure. The sales manager is paid, not to set objectives, but to achieve results.

However, all results, to be accomplished, need to be compared to some standard, some yardstick—to have some means by which success or failure can be measured. "To maintain harmonious customer relations" is certainly an enviable goal. How do you judge whether this has been satisfactorily achieved? Ask both the salesman and the sales manager if the salesman has satisfactorily achieved this objective of the job. "Certainly," the salesman replies. "This is one of my strengths in developing the accounts I'm responsible for." "Very good," counters the manager. "However, I noticed you do not call weekly on your major buyers."

Who is correct? Why, they both are! And simply because they are both seeing the function of the job from the viewpoint of their individual perceptions. That is the end result of management by objectives (MBO) or the corporate appraisal system tied to specific short-term objectives—which means that in one quick stroke, we have tied together everything that has been discussed under the subject of setting objectives, supervision and control, and using the appraisal system for your own control purposes rather than merely for a salary review. This is everything we discussed through Chapter 5. How can these concepts be considered separately and still give direction to a management system?

> Ed Smith says, "As a part of what we have discussed during this salary review, let's set the following objective: 'To call weekly on each major purchaser.'" (I do not care whether this specific objective is or is not reasonable. They agree to it, and it is measurable.)

And the point is, having the objective changes a lot of things. It becomes a tool for supervision and control; it becomes something to attain. And if it also results in developing additional business, it reduces the "gap." Finally, if this is what the sales manager sincerely feels will result in sales success, it is a criterion to be looked for in the selection process. We have now folded together all of the first five chapters.

If I had stopped right there, I would probably have touched on most of the areas that mean success or failure for the sales manager. Yet even if this point represented 95 percent, why shouldn't the goal be 120 percent effectiveness? Being the best you can be thus became the continuing objective of the balance of the book.

The Professional Sales Manager

Pros are good at what they do. They know why they do what they do—and are always striving to improve themselves. A manager's style is an instinctive style. Each of us began developing that style from our earliest years, from association with peers, teachers, and our first boss. Yet if we remain open to the world around us, we never stop learning; we never stop stretching and growing. This is what being a professional means. Yet at no moment can the manager stand independent of the people he is responsible for—the sales force. The manager's success comes only through their successes. Their failures are his failures.

Quality circles, originally an American innovation, do not fail as a concept: It is people (management) who fail the concept. Many of the concepts espoused in the quality circles approach apply to the elements of building a sales team outlined in Chapter 6. At no point was it suggested that a sales manager could not achieve success without applying these concepts. What was said was that through an understanding of these concepts, the sales manager would be in a better position to contribute to the individual and combined growth of those who reported to him or her. What was said was that by the conscious application of these principles, the sales manager could develop the good sales force into the effective sales force. While Chapter 6 presented the concepts, Chapter 7 discussed how the sales manager could use them, how the manager's style could affect the output, the effectiveness, of the sales force.

However, even these chapters do not stand alone. No team effectiveness effort can be successful unless it is built on the basic concepts established in the earlier chapters. Thus, while we could have stopped after Chapter 5 and said, "This is what you need to be a successful sales manager," we could not have stopped there and been able to say, "You are as effective as you can be."

Training ties together the knowledge, skill, and attitude of the professional salesman. Yet training, as we saw, is not something left to the trainers. *No one can train a salesman to sell.* The sole objective of training is to show salespeople how to think. The value of sales experience was never disputed, yet it was recognized that the salesman who is forced to learn by experience alone cannot compete with the salesman whose learning is the result of both his experience and a planned, coordinated training program. Experience is what the salesman uses to apply the techniques and skills presented in the seminars and workshops to the real situation on the job.

The misapplication of these skills, techniques, and training concepts lies at the heart of sales failure. Salesmen fail for many reasons, some their own. But the impact of the trained, thinking, knowledgeable sales manager can often turn failure into success. Sales managers cannot change history, but they can have a positive impact on the future if they can properly read the present and see what is needed. They can give direction to the future.

Just what is it that is needed? Sometimes this, sometimes that. Only a proverbial Solomon could sit in judgment on any particular present situation and decree an absolute corrective action. Few of us qualify for the role of Solomon. We can, however, set the stage by knowing what is needed to measure success. What is the "gap"? What will it take to close it? How do I assure those results? How do I measure their achievement? What does it take to be an effective sales manager? This is what I have tried to tell you through my own experience and the experiences of the many other sales managers I have known and who thus contributed unwittingly to these pages—advice from manager to manager.

And Go for the Gold!

But I assume you want this to be the beginning of your own management career, not just a way station, regardless of how successful that might be. You want to grow toward being a truly professional manager. Pros, as noted earlier, are good at what they do—they know why they do what they do. (This is the manager-to-manager advice you have found in this book.) *They know that their future growth comes from this constant learning.* There is only one word of advice regarding this: Take every opportunity to learn. Read, talk to those who have already achieved, be open to new experiences, and learn from them what you need in order to be better the next time.

The late Vince Lombardi (ignore the positive and negative aspects of his personality) was an acknowledged developer of those for whom he was responsible. In his own words:

> I will demand a commitment to excellence; that is what life is all about, and that is the job of the leader. Many mornings when I am worried or depressed I have to give myself a pep talk, because I am not going before that ball club without being able to exude assurance. I must be the first believer, because there is no way you can hoodwink the players.

The entire effort and direction of this book has concentrated on what the new sales manager should do to ensure success. At the same time, failure is always no more than the flip side of the coin. Simply stated, if these steps represent success, the absence of these steps represents, if not failure, at least mediocrity.

Unfortunately, we can fail in other ways—perhaps not the type of failure that sends us hurtling back down one whole evolutionary level, but the small differences that separate the merely good from the professional.

Aristotle wrote: "and as in the olympic games, it is not the most beautiful and the strongest that are crowned but those who compete—for it is of these that come the victorious. So those who act win, and rightly win." In February of 1980, at the Winter Olympics in Lake Placid, a group of previously unknown American hockey players beat the highly-trained Russian team 5 to 4 and won for themselves the opportunity to beat Finland the next Sunday and capture a gold medal. As a sports writer commented at the time, if they had not managed to beat Finland that Sunday, then the defeat of the Russian team, as tremendous as that was, would have meant nothing. Managing is a lot like that. All of the principles and techniques of sales management are meaningless if they do not re-

sult in obtaining targeted, profitable sales. Being effective and efficient is what we are paid for as managers.

All managers are faced with both uncontrollable and controllable factors that will affect the management concepts they apply.
Managers do not primarily seek to solve a single problem once and
for all or to achieve a single objective. Some problems can be solved
quickly and easily, while others require a long-term effort. Still
other problems must be kept under control but can never be fully
solved. To succeed as a manager, you must be able to deal with *all*
of these types of problems.

I do not know what it is that makes the difference. I don't
know, and maybe I never will. Perhaps the managers who succeed
have some recurring dream about perfecting themselves, about living up to some damned image always a little out of reach. But they
try. They reach out and fall and get up and reach some more until
they succeed, and the organization grows a little.

I do not think managers seek problems to solve, yet somehow
problems find us because that is the nature of being a manager.
When the problems come, we react to them, and the problems
hopefully disappear, while leaving us with the imprint of what we
have experienced, of how we have responded. The behavioral
people tell us that our reactions are not wholly determined by
forces within us. Just like an electrical appliance, we are "turned
on" and "turned off" by stimuli that lie outside us. We can only
respond to what we see or hear. We see a problem, take action, and
watch and listen to the result of that action. What is crucial is the
clarity with which we see the oncoming problem that we will respond to. Likewise, our perception of the departing event has a
great influence on the way we will solve similar problems in the
future. It establishes our perception of the way the system in which
we work functions.

A basic premise of this book is the need for sales managers to
develop their conceptual skills: to learn to see what is happening in
the business world of which they are a part—and to see the role
they play in an ever larger circle that is the corporation. Problems
are only effectively solved if they can be related to causes, which
may at times be external to the problem itself.

There are four criteria for choosing the best from among the
available solutions to any problem—four criteria that have a specific and special significance when applied to the role of the new
sales manager:

1. Determine the risk you face with each option open to you. There is never a riskless action, nor often a riskless "inaction." Doing nothing to solve a problem is merely one of the choices open to you.
2. Determine which course of action carries with it the least chance of disturbing the status quo. Change is often an option when one is choosing a solution to any problem, and at times, the sales manager will find change necessary. However, all the management books and articles notwithstanding, the new sales manager is particularly cautioned to move carefully in this area. Know your facts, and look for your boss to champion the move—or otherwise, abandon it and find a less disruptive means to the same end.
3. Determine the urgency of the decision. Will the business or the sales group be harmed if an immediate decision is not forthcoming?
4. Determine what limitations exist in the resources you will need to carry out your choice of a solution. A decision will be no better than the ability of the people who will be called on to execute it.

"The purpose of a business," says Peter Drucker, "is to create a customer." The sales force accomplish this by satisfying needs and are rewarded with an order. Since this seldom happens automatically in the corporate scheme of things, someone or some group must be responsible for making it happen. This is the role of the sales manager. The manager adds meaning to the purpose of the corporate entity by determining what will be done to obtain that customer; by deciding who will perform what tasks to secure that customer; by making sure those performing the various tasks are doing their best in their assigned areas; and finally, by making sure all the other parts of the corporation are going to come together at the right time to secure that customer. Thus, it is in the nature of the sales management function that sales managers plan, organize, staff, motivate, and control that part of the corporation for which their superiors, in their infinite wisdom, have made them responsible.

Fortunately, effective management can be learned. In fact, it must be learned. Some years ago, I had the opportunity and pleasure of participating in a discussion in which the topic was "How does the manager become effective?" It was an interesting discussion, primarily because of the range of viewpoints expressed by the various managers participating. Among the conclusions expressed by the more academic members of the group was that most managers would do practically anything to become better managers except use the rules that could make them better managers.

This is not hard to understand. Modern management theorists are overenamored with the tools of the trade. However, the tools of management are like those of the fisherman. Even with the right lure and the correct methods, you don't automatically get results. On the contrary, as in selecting that "right" lure, this is only a small part of the task. Nothing would please the manager more than successful "management by principle and rule." Unfortunately, managers are paid, not for doing what is academically right, but for getting the right thing done.

Truly effective management is a continuing, never ending process learned under the pressures of the firing line. Successful managers do use those tools that have proved themselves in the heat of battle; they do learn from those who have gone before them. However, even champion golfers do not use every club in their bag in every game. What is important is that golfers know which club will serve them best in a particular situation. That comes from experience at the game and also from knowing the course being played. Just as champion golfers make use of all the techniques of their game, champions on the management course make use of all the techniques of their game. They plan, they organize, they motivate, and they control. Functions are as inherently intertwined and inseparable in management as on the golf circuit. No manager can be efficient and effective by neglecting any single function. You don't lie six strokes to the green and say, "Now for a good putt!"

Managers plan. The essence of planning is goal-oriented, and a crucial first step in the planning process is the establishment of objectives. As Peter Drucker has pointed out, "the objectives of an organization are management objectives." The primary management function at all levels is setting the goals of the organization or unit. The goals establish the basis for planning. Planning, looking at the long range as well as the short range, is essential to the survival not only of the company but of the individual sales unit.

Sales force direction and growth, in terms of developing customers, present the manager with a never ending variety of "opportunities." Without planning, the elements that make up the manager's unit of responsibility end up being run through some variation of "management by fear," "management by directive," "management by mucilage and bailing wire," or "management by meat ax." With planning, the sales manager brings with him, not chaos, but an informed, direction-oriented "management by objectives."

Managers organize and staff. From sound, goal-directed planning comes the development of the structure that will support those plans. At the same time, the essence of organization is the development of the needs and personal objectives of the salespeople who compose the organization.

Managers motivate. Management is defined as the process of reaching organizational goals by working through and with the resources of that organization. One of the most valuable, least developed, and changeable resources of any organization is its people. We don't manage things; we manage emotions. The manager is the catalyst for moving the people in the organization efficiently and effectively toward making things happen.

One sales force is not more effective than another because it consists of better salespeople who are higher-paid, better-trained, or more skilled. But one sales force will have better people because the spirit, which is a management spirit, has created the motivation for growth and self-development. People become effective when they are led by effectiveness. The imprint a manager puts on his sales unit creates the environment that leads to better-motivated salesmen.

Managers control. The basis for corporate growth lies in the unifying sense of direction a firm's management creates through its planning. Top management defines the philosophy of what the firm is in business for—its purpose for existing—and establishes a direction for the organization to follow. But all managers can fail for their own reasons. They can spend so much time solving their own immediate, short-run problems that they never have time to tie their own planning in to corporate goals. They resort to "management by fire in the paint locker." On the other hand, they can be so involved with the environment that is the total corporation that they somehow fail to see the fact that what they have so wondrously planned for their own department never gets done. Without direction and the proper day-to-day supervision and control, failure will only be a matter of time.

Because business is exposed to the dynamics of a relatively un-controllable environment, managers seldom have the opportunity to apply the same management principles and techniques twice to an identical or even a very similar problem. Throughout the planning, the organizing, the motivating, and the controlling, the aware manager must be constantly on the alert to recognize the different, changing variables that will affect his approach. It is not the management principles or techniques that must be flexible and capable of being changed to meet such varying conditions but rather the manager. The successful sales manager knows how to make use both of the principles of management and of his own experiences in meeting the challenge of new situations. This is the ultimate art of management. This is what makes management a unique art. Principles give you the rules of the game—experience shows you when and how to bend the rules. But you do so with full awareness that a part of every manager's position description reads, "Total responsibility, commensurate authority, and all inherent danger!"

"Ladies and gentlemen, this is your captain speaking. We have just been cleared for our final approach. Please fasten your seat belts and extinguish all smoking materials until you are well inside the terminal."

Thus we end this portion of your journey into the functions and functioning of sales management. Know where you are going. Find and develop good salespeople whose strength lies in the knowledge and skills of the selling game. Keep your objectives always in front of you like a banner. Here are the principles and tools for a new sales manager's survival.

Good luck—and good selling!

Index

achievement motivation, 144
activity reporting, 70–79
    see also key-negotiation summary
Advanced Industrial Selling (Stumm), 80
American Management Association, 134
Argyris, Chris, 121, 125–126, 143–144
appraisal interview, see performance appraisal interview
appraisal system, see performance appraisal system
Aristotle, on competition, 223
audiovisual equipment for presentations, 168–170
authority, delegating, 90–91

behavior, psychology of
    management style and, 144–155
    maturity levels in, 149–154
    organizational, 141–144
    temperament theory in, 134–141
behavior relationship grid, 144–146
Blake, Dr. Robert R., 122, 134
budget(s)
    as cost control, 61–62, 85–89
    cost function in, 64–65
    definition of, 60–61
    as effectiveness measurement, 63
    elements of, 63–64
    as management tool, 62
    as sales control, 62
buying process as failure factor, 203–205

call-planning report, 70–79, 125
    see also key-negotiation summary
call report, 69–70, 125
"change index," 3, 5
committed costs, 63–64
communicating
    in company, 3–6, 94–97, 130–131
    one-on-one, 10–11
    with superiors, 10–11
    see also behavior, psychology of; management style
company policy
    interpreting, 5, 6
    objectives and, 54–57
"conscientiousness" temperament, 135, 139, 140–141, 146
consultants, training, 189–190
contact code, 74

control, methods of, 92–97, 227–228
see also supervising function
cooperative-motivation system, 128, 129–130
cost control, budget as, 61–62, 85–89
cost function, measuring, 64–65
criteria for selection interview, 25–26, 33–36, 41–46
criteria for solutions, 224–225
customer categorization, 50–51

Dangerous Currents (Thurow), 118
delegation, art of, 89–92
direction as management purpose, 6–7
discrimination in selection process, 45–46
"dominance" temperament, 135, 136–137, 139–140, 146, 149–151, 153
Drucker, Peter, 54, 225, 226
Dyer, David, 118

Economics, Peace, and Laughter (Galbraith), 93
Eisenhower, Dwight D., as leader, 93
Emotions of Normal People (Geier), 122, 135
employee annual appraisal system, see performance appraisal system
employment ad in selection process, 47–48
environment
creating positive, 19–21, 94–97, 133
"hygiene factors" in, 144
interpreting, see behavior, psychology of
see also management style
expense trends, territory, 87–89

failure factors, sales, 195–215
Fiedler, F., 123
firing employees, 112–113
5 percent competitive solution, 199–200
"force-field analysis," 147–149
forecast, budget, 60–61
formal sales training programs, 184–194

Galbraith, John Kenneth, 93
"gap" approach, 12–15, 53
developing strategies for, 15–19, 21–22
see also territory objectives
Geier, Dr. John, 122, 134, 135
Gellerman, Saul, 121
Geneen, Harold, 126
generic training programs, 190–191

halo effect as interview error, 36–37
"Hawthorne effect," 141
Herzberg, Frederick, 144
heuristic balancing, 51
high-"C" temperament, 139, 140–141, 146
high-"D" temperament, 136–137, 139–140, 146, 149–151, 153
high-"I" temperament, 137–138, 140, 146, 150–151
high-"S" temperament, 138, 140, 146, 154
hiring, see selection process
House, Robert J., 123

"Influence: A Key to Effective Leadership" (Peltz), Personnel, 130
"influencing" temperament, 137–138, 140, 146, 150–151
Institute for Social Research (University of Michigan), 120–121, 124, 125

interview, appraisal, *see* performance appraisal interview
interview, selection, *see* selection process

job description, 25–26, 33–36, 101, 104–106
job-related system, 128–129
Johnson, Thomas, 124

key-account strategy, 79–87
key-negotiation summary, 79–87

language of selling, 178–180
Lawrence, Paul, 118
Leadership and Motivation (McGregor), 121
leadership behavior, *see* management style
Likert, Rensis, 120–121, 124, 125, 128, 144–146
Lombardi, Vince, on leadership, 223

managed costs, 64
manager, *see* sales manager
Management and Organizational Development (Argyris), 121
Management by Motivation (Gellerman), 121
management by objectives system, *see* MBO system
management control, *see* supervising function
management style
  behavioral theories and, 144–145
  communications effect and, 130–131
  flexibility in, 154–155
  group maturity and, 125–127
  ideal, 122–124
  job-related system and, 128–129
  team building and, 127–128

see also behavior, psychology of; sales training program(s)
management team building, 119–131
  see also management style
Managerial Grid® seminar, 122, 134
Marston, Dr. William, 134, 135
Massey, Dr. Morris, 116
maturity levels in sales force, 149–154
Mayo, Elton, 141
MBO (management by objectives) system
  creating, 8–23
  environment, positive, for, 19–21
  "gap" approach as, 12–15, 53
  performance appraisal and, 98–101, 103–106
  territory strategies as, 15–19
  see also call-planning report; performance appraisal system; territory objectives
McClelland, David, 144
McGregor, Douglas, 115, 121, 124–125, 141–143, 144
meeting-room necessities, 160
Merrill, Dr. David, 134, 139
motivation
  creating, 19–21, 94–97, 114–131, 132–133, 227
  factors, 144
  see also behavior, psychology of; management style
Motivation of the Engineer (Pelz), 126
Mouton, Dr. Jane S., 122, 134

need
  acceptance, 206–207
  communication barriers and, 207–209
  establishing, 205–215

need (*continued*)
  psychology of, 205–206
  selling, 206
  techniques for selling, 209–215
negotiation stage, 79–87
New Patterns of Management
  (Likert), 120

objectives, *see* MBO system; short-
  term objectives; territory objectives
one-on-one communication, 10–11
on-the-job coaching, 176–184
organizational behavior theories,
  141–155
organizational strategies, developing, 211–215
  see also team building, management

participative management, 119–
  131
*Path-Goal Theory of Leader Effec-
  tiveness, A* (House), 123
"Path-Goal Theory of Leadership,
  The" (Stinson and Johnson),
  Management Journal, 124
peer discussion, 127
Pelz, D.C., 126, 130
performance appraisal interview
  conducting, 106–111
  preparing for, 103–106
  salesperson's side of, 102–103
performance appraisal system
  firing in, 112–113
  interview in, 102–111
  management by objectives as,
    98–101
  standards in, 112
  traditional approaches to, 101–
    102
Performax International, 134

personal-comfort considerations
  for sales meetings, 161–167
Peters, M. K. "Pete," 4
physical arrangements, sales meeting, 157–160
position description, 25–26, 33–
  36, 101, 104–106
presentations
  material details for, 167–172
  seating arrangements for, 158–
    160
productive measuring, *see* performance appraisal system
"productivity crisis," 117–118
Psychological Associates of St.
  Louis, 134
Psychological Service of Pittsburgh, 144

quality circles, 118

reference checks in selection process, 47
Renewing American Industry
  (Lawrence and Dyer), 118
responsibility, delegating and re-
  taining, 91–92
résumé data, analyzing, 26–34

salary review programs, 101–102
  see also performance appraisal
    system
sales calls, *see* call-planning report;
  key-negotiation summary
sales control, budget, 62, 85–87
sales failure factors, 195–215
Sales Grid® seminar, 122, 134
sales itinerary planning, 74–75
sales manager
  professional, 221–228
  transition from salesman to, 2–
    7, 20–23

see also management style; supervising function
sales meetings
   checklist for, 172–174
   material-presentation details for,
      167–172
   personal-comfort considerations
      for, 161–167
   physical arrangements for, 157–
      160
sales objectives, *see* call-planning
   report; MBO system; territory
   objectives
sales training program(s)
   failure of, 198–199
   formal, 184–194
   on-the-job coaching as, 176–184
seating arrangements for sales
   meetings, 157–160
selection process
   beginning the, 37–43
   criteria for, 25–26, 33–36, 41–
      43
   discrimination in, 45–46
   employment ad in, 47–48
   final choice in, 43–45
   interview in, 24–43
   reference checks in, 47
service, selling as, 200–202
short-term objectives, setting, 99–
      101, 108–109, 111
   see also MBO system
solution criteria, 224–225
staffing up, *see* selection process
standards, setting
   in performance appraisal, 112
   for training programs, 186–188
"steadiness" temperament, 138,
      140, 146, 154
Stinson, John, 123–124
strategies, organizational, 211–215
strategies, sales, *see* call-planning
   report; key-account strategy;

sales training program(s); territory objectives
supervising function, 68–97
   call-planning as, 70–79
   control, methods of, as, 93–97,
      227–228
   delegation, art of, as, 89–92
   key-account strategy as, 79–87
   summary of, 226–228
   territory expense trends, track-
      ing, as, 87–89
   see also management style; per-
      formance appraisal system;
      sales training program(s)
"supportive relationship," 124

team building, management, 119–
      131, *see also* management
      style
temperament theory, 134–141
territory expense trends, tracking,
      87–89
territory management
   customer categorization and,
      50–51
   expense trends and, 87–89
   travel logistics and, 51–52
   see also call-planning report
territory objectives
   budgets and, 58–66
   developing, 15–19
   "gap" approach and, 53
   nature of, 54–57
   setting, 57–58
   see also call-planning report
Theories X and Y, 115, 124–125,
      141–143
*Theory of Leadership Effective-
   ness, A,* (Fiedler), 123
Third Wave, The, (Toffler), 118
Thurow, Lester, 118
Toffler, Alvin, 118

Tracom Corporation, 134, 139
training consultants, 189–190
training needs, determining, 186–
    188
training programs, sales, *see* sales
    training program(s)
travel itinerary, 70–79, 125
travel logistics, 51–52, 74–75
Type A and B behavior, 143

unsupported hunch as interview
    error, 36–37
upward communication, impor-
    tance of, 10–11

visual materials for presentations,
    170–172

Westinghouse, 4, 195